G. ERIC PACE
with Dorothy Lois Lissner

DON'T JUST SIT THERE—LIVE

Achieving
SUCCESS
and
HAPPINESS

PERENNIAL LIBRARY
Harper & Row, Publishers
New York, Hagerstown, San Francisco, London

To
an outstanding teacher,
Dr. Raymond Charles Barker

This book was originally published in 1976 by Deerpark Press.
It is here reprinted by arrangement with the authors.

First PERENNIAL LIBRARY edition published 1977

ISBN: 0–06–080422–X

79 80 81   10 9 8 7 6 5 4 3 2

CONTENTS

Contents

CHAPTER I

Science of Mind: Technique
for Success and Happiness

No way? Sure there's a way! If you've been a constant failure you can become a constant success. If you're poor you can prosper. If you're lonely, have no friends and feel nobody could possibly love you, you can make friends and achieve loving relationships. If you're out of a job, hate your work or don't seem to be reaching your highest potential, you can change any of these conditions.

Or if you're just searching but don't know what you're searching for, you can find the something for which you're looking, the place you fit into, the role that's right for you.

How? Well, I'll tell you how I did it and if I could do it you certainly can too. It isn't a matter of the breaks or will power. It's a matter of learning certain principles and applying a technique based on them — both of which I am going to explain to you very simply — principles and a technique that I believe anyone can understand and apply, even though they come from the frontiers of science and philosophy.

What are these principles, this technique? The principles are the basic ideas in something called Science of Mind. The technique, called treatment, is the method of applying them.

And when I discovered them both they changed my entire life.

They also relieved me of a chronic, debilitating disease, diabetes, that threatened that life, although I hadn't been looking for anything so miraculous. But only because it had never occurred to me that such a thing was even remotely possible.

I didn't achieve this astonishing healing overnight. It took months of study and effort, many months when hope alternated with despair, many months when advances followed setbacks and setbacks succeeded advances. Did I get discouraged? Of course I did. Did I think of quitting? Often. But once I was convinced of the truth of the principles behind Science of Mind it was no longer possible for me to consider seriously giving up.

Fundamental to this science is the idea that your experiences mirror your consciousness, your state of mind. If you want to change your circumstances, the conditions of your life, then you have to change your consciousness. Which means that you must change the inner state of your thoughts and feelings if you want to change the outer conditions and affairs, the happenings in your world.

This process of changing your consciousness is what I've just called treatment (which has nothing to do with medicine). It consists of conscious retraining of the subconscious mind — and, as I've said, I firmly believe that that retraining can be learned by anyone who reads and studies and applies the information in this book.

Science has always known that change of any kind is produced by a creative law of cause and effect. Situations, conditions, relationships, forms are the results of our thoughts. Beliefs, attitudes, habits, emotions, perceptions and patterns of thought are causes of the situations, conditions, relationships and forms in our present existence. The way we change results is by changing causes.

Redirecting the subconscious mind and redirecting it effectively is what the technique of Science of Mind is all about. We are determining what we want to experience by putting conscious, rational choices into the creative mind within us. We are freeing ourselves from having to accept what happens to us as a result of our past choices, conscious or subconscious, or of the past choices which we accepted from others.

The technique of Science of Mind can be used in all areas of life. It can be used to maintain or restore health. It can be used to improve finances and solve money problems. It can be used to acquire love and intimate social relationships, which all human beings want and are entitled to. It can be used to employ one's talents and abilities at their highest level, to discover and foster all one's potentials for self-expression. In other words, the study and application of Science of Mind can help, whatever the problem, whatever the need. All human endeavor, in fact, can be said to fall into one of these categories, health, money, love and self-expression and later in this book I shall discuss each of them individually and in depth.

We start making rational choices and getting what we desire. We stop making irrational choices and taking what befalls us. Am I saying that I once chose to be a diabetic? No, but I did harbor subconscious thoughts and emotions which produce diabetes, although I had no knowledge of that fact when I first discovered that I had the illness.

Here's what happened. Almost without warning, one day when I was twenty-four, my appendix suddenly ruptured. When they got me to the emergency ward for an appendectomy the doctors discovered that I had a critical case of diabetes — something I'd not suspected. It was so critical, in fact, that they had to put me on insulin every three hours and that's a lot of insulin.

Now, at the time I was a dancer on Broadway and it may sound silly but I was less concerned with the threat to my life than I was with the threat to my career. I loved dance and I was determined I was never going to stop dancing.

I was back on stage six weeks after I had the ruptured appendix.

I had gotten over the appendectomy in six weeks but the diabetes was still there.

What to do? Well, of course, there was nothing to do except keep taking insulin and go on being determined that the diabetes wasn't going to stop me from dancing.

The determination paid off — as far as the dancing was concerned. I eventually did stop but only on the stage and only to start directing plays.

So the diabetes wasn't threatening to shorten my career any more. Just to shorten my life.

Meanwhile I was also searching for something. I didn't know for what. It wasn't anything I could have stated in words. I studied Hinduism and Hatha Yoga, which is the exercises, the beginning training in Indian mysticism. It's to teach one's body to get out of the way so one can meditate. I was trained privately and, luckily, by a wonderful person.

And I studied psychology at the five colleges I attended at one time or another. Wherever I went on tour I jumped in and studied. I never cared about degrees which is interesting, now that I think about it. I just wanted to study and I always studied whatever I wanted to study. Here, too, searching. Here, too, not knowing for what.

At times I was doing a number of things simultaneously, dancing, going to college, teaching dance. One year I went to San Francisco to teach a summer session of dance and I began studying at San Francisco State and just stayed for two years. I worked my way through those two years of college by running a dance school. I had to. I had no savings then and of course I had to support myself. So I rented the American Legion Hall in Los Altos twice a week and went there and taught children.

When I wasn't studying or working I was looking further afield for the something I thought might give me an answer. The year I was at the university in Perugia, Italy, I made several trips to Assisi, six miles away, to see the Franciscan friars there, and I can remember thinking, If only I could be a Franciscan. But then I would think of the theology and know I couldn't be, although I had been brought up a Catholic.

One summer I was producing a summer theatre program in Santa Cruz and I went to the mission there. An appeal had gone out for Brothers. And I thought, If only I could answer this call to be one of the Brothers.

But I couldn't.

The following year somebody took me to hear a lecture at the Society for Psychical Research in New York City. That's when I began to discover psychic phenomena. I chased around to all the spiritualist churches in the city that year and to all the mediums I could find. I became aware of Tarot cards. I read all the Jess Stearn books. I read all the books that are in the 133.3 section of the public library. I learned about the search for Bridey Murphy.

This last sort of thing appealed to me. I'd think, Ah, this is the scientific way. These are psychologists trying to discover proof of reincarnation.

Could this be what I was looking for? I wondered.

Six years after my appendectomy I had a period — I was travelling around the country with the national company of "Inherit the Wind" — when I took to visiting a lot of Greek and Russian Orthodox churches. I can't explain why, except as part of the search. I'd visit the main cathedrals wherever I went. In San Francisco I attended the Russian Orthodox church a number of times. I found the separation of the men from the women strange. I toyed with the idea of going into Greek Orthodoxy. It had never interested me before. I'd drop into a Greek church and people would speak to me in Greek and I'd have to shake my head, tell them in English that I was just a visitor and couldn't speak their language.

Searching. Always searching.

And not finding. Still not really knowing what I was looking for. Or why I was looking at all.

Because I wasn't bothered by any big emotional problems, at least I didn't think I was, as others I met who were also searching often seem to be. I had a burdensome physical ailment but, as I said, I wasn't trying to find a cure. Mainly because I didn't think there was any cure. By then I had enough money so I wasn't feeling any great pinch. I was doing all right as far as jobs and using my talents and abilities were concerned. By the time I was thirty I had achieved a place in the theatre far beyond my original goal. I had become production assistant in a big Broadway show, starring Paul Muni, "Inherit the Wind," the same show I was later to accompany on the road when Melvyn Douglas took over the stellar role.

All in all I was a success beyond my wildest dreams. Still, I did have a kind of loneliness.

But it wasn't that I lacked friends. I don't mean that. I could have been busy night and day. It's that I had a kind of basic loneliness.

And then I hit another spell of what I call "meandering." It had happened to me twice before in my life. I'd discover I was wandering around with everything seemingly right and yet I wasn't right. I'd take to walking the streets by myself. Or I'd be at a theatre bar with a group of twenty people or more and I'd be talking and laughing and abruptly I'd break off, thinking, If I could just get out of here . . . . I have to get out of here. Away. By myself.

I was a success but everything seemed to be dull, without meaning.

Well, that's how it was with me. I was just kind of meandering around when I saw a big ad in the New York Times. The ad was about a book by a man named Donald Curtis, "Your Thoughts Can Change Your Life." I didn't know who Donald Curtis was. I didn't know anything about the book. I had never sent for a book from any newspaper before and I never have since.

But for some reason I was impelled to send for that book. And when it came I felt impelled to begin reading it immediately. I did and read straight through, without stopping.

6

He wrote about Science of Mind and the place where it was taught in New York City. I was surprised as I suddenly realized, Why that's that funny little gray building, across from City Center, the place that used to be a carriage house.

I had seen it many times but had never been very curious about it.

I didn't finish reading until late that night. The next day as soon as I had a free moment I rushed to the phone, called the building and asked the person who answered when another lecture was scheduled.

"There's a talk going on in about 15 minutes," I was told.

"I'll be there," I said. "I can make it. I live within walking distance."

I hung up, totally unconscious of how peculiar I must have sounded.

I did make it. I heard the talk and I was fascinated.

As I slowly returned to my apartment I thought to myself, I'll keep going back. I'll keep listening to what they have to say. I think maybe they have something.

It turned out that for me they did. Science of Mind not only brought a remission of my diabetes but satisfactorily ended my search for meaning to my life. In fact, eventually, I gave up my profession in the theatre to become a lecturer, a writer and a counselor in the teaching.

CHAPTER II

Use It for Health,

Love, Peace

Eight years later . . . .
He sat across the desk from me and told me that he thought
he was cracking up. He was a big man, easily six feet, but he
was shrunk in on himself and quivering as if he were a small,
helpless child.

"I'd about decided to put myself in some hospital to get
psychiatric help. Then Bob — Bob Palmer — I think you
know him. He's a student in one of your classes."

I nodded.

"Well, anyway, Bob's in the same office as I am and
when he saw I was just like teetering on the edge, he suggested I come to the noon lecture. Hear you speak. I did.
Then I made this appointment. Can you help me?"

"I can teach you how to help yourself. The same way I
learned to help myself."

"I don't want to put myself away because I've got a wife
and two little girls and they need me." He paused and appeared to reconsider. "Or maybe they don't. Oh, I don't
know. I'm no good to them the way I am. I'm filled with fear.
I can't sleep. I can't eat. I can hardly work. I'm terrified I'm

going to get fired and then what will we do? I'm a total failure."

A total failure? This young, handsome man whose custom-made suit and bearing — except for the posture and drooping shoulders — gave every indication of his being what I later found he actually was, a thirty-five thousand dollar a year executive?

I had learned much about the vagaries of the human mind in the years since I first entered the funny little gray building on 55th Street. Now it has been torn down and a big, modern, many-windowed skyscraper stands in its place. And, having given up my career in dancing, producing and directing in the midst of a long line of successes, I was now a teacher in the new Science of Mind headquarters a number of blocks to the south. I had found what I was searching for and I felt compelled to teach it to others who were searching as I had once searched.

But that's my personal story. I'll tell you more about it later. For the moment I only want to explain how I happened to be sitting in a counselor's office on the fourth floor, across the desk from a young man so desperate he was considering committing himself to a hospital for the mentally ill.

"Tell me more about this fear," I prompted him. "Or fears. Whichever. What are you afraid of?"

"Oh . . . . I'm not sure. Everything. I mean, there's so many of them."

He frowned as he struggled to clarify his thoughts. "My father died of a heart attack. He was only twenty-nine. I was eight. I guess I've always been afraid since then. Yes, that's it. It started then. I'm afraid of death. Terrified is actually the word. And, of course, I'm afraid of getting sick. Of being alone. Of losing my job. Of — everything. Everything. A cold. The least little thing. If I have a twitch in my big toe I get in a panic."

He smiled painfully. "I joke but it's no joke. Believe me, it's no joke. And it's not something I can control. I try. Believe me I try.

9

"But that's not all. I'm a rotten husband and father."

"Oh," I said. "In what way?"

"I don't make enough money. Not for my family. My wife — she's used to more. A lot more. I ought to have a better job. I'm in marketing but I'm one of four in my department. I could do what the department head does but I'll never get the chance. Not so long as I stay with the company I'm working for. And I'm not up to trying to find another job somewhere else. I'm too afraid. I couldn't make out in an interview. Couldn't sell myself. All that. I couldn't sell myself as a street cleaner right now. Though I'm well qualified for what I do and it shouldn't be any problem."

His voice broke. "I'm a real big failure. I'm a complete flop."

We were back to where we'd started and it was to be some time before I could say to him one day, "You know, Neal, I haven't heard you say you're a failure recently. We're making progress."

By that time he was able to grin and the strain was gone from his face. He didn't answer but he and I both knew that, regardless of how often he might be assailed by doubts, he was never going to think of himself as a failure again. And not just because he was well on the way to becoming the very successful man he now is. Today he heads a department in another, much larger, company and is making more than enough money to meet the needs of his family and the standards of his wife.

Is he absolutely free of all his fears? No, one or another crops up now and then. But he keeps working to be free of them and he's confident he's going to get rid of them entirely some day.

And that's good enough for him and it's good enough for me. Because meanwhile he can handle them. They don't throw him anymore. He can function and function very well.

As a result of our talks he saw a doctor, went through a series of tests, got a clean bill of health and has taped it to the mirror where he shaves every day. To remind him that he's healthy. So if his toe happens to twitch he says to himself emphatically, Nothing's wrong. Nothing can possibly be wrong. I'm 100 per cent healthy. I've got the tests to prove it. Taped to my bathroom mirror. I'm absolute, total health.

His fear of death? He got over that. He knows he's going to die like the rest of us but he doesn't expect it to be soon. He's come to accept that birth and death follow a natural law, a law of this earth plane of action. We arrive on this plane by birth and we leave it by death. We are born at the right time for us and we leave at the right time for us and the leaving doesn't have to be at the termination of a catastrophic illness. It doesn't have to be associated with illness at all — that's just an idea that's been handed on from one generation to another. It can be an altogether peaceful transition.

I encounter miracles in my work but not often, in the sense that we think of miracles, which is to say an immediate, dramatic change. Mostly change, great change, takes a little time. But the important thing is that I do encounter change. Every day. In all areas of people's lives. Failures like Neal become successes. Ill people, seriously ill people, as I once was, become well. Men and women wanting to get married find someone to love and marry. Unhappy people become happy. Poor people become prosperous. People begin to learn and understand the process we call creative living. They begin living dynamic, self-fulfilling lives. They don't just drag through an 'allotted time.'

And many of these people do it without any more help than you can get from the pages of this book. Occasionally, of course, someone like Neal finds himself in a situation where he's unable to cope adequately and so he comes to me or someone like me to work with him.

Incidentally Neal has a cousin in another city who is a psychoanalyst and not long ago the cousin said, "I don't know what you're doing, Neal, but whatever it is, stick with it. You say it's not psychiatry. Well . . . . Anyhow, I guess I have to admit that I couldn't have done for you in three years what this thing did for you in eight months."

For every person, like Neal, who feels he or she has to get help I have scores of individuals I know only through letters and hundreds of students whom I've never seen outside of one of the many regular classes I teach each week. Or at least who have never visited my office. They come to the lectures, master the technique and apply it, set goals for themselves and achieve these goals on their own.

Applying the technique is just as important as knowing it; actually, knowing it is of little value if you don't apply it.

Frequently, though, students are so excited — especially the newcomers — by the astonishing things that have begun to happen in their lives that they seek me out after a class or during intermission to share some of them with me.

One of the most interesting accounts was told to me after a noon lecture recently by a slight, intense woman. She had been sitting by herself in a rear corner of the auditorium and as I walked down the aisle she started toward me. I could tell by the expression on her face that she was anxious to talk to me but as I approached where she stood, numbers of students began as usual to attach themselves to me, calling out greetings, questions, bits and pieces of information.

When she saw that I was all but surrounded she turned away and retreated into one of the rows of seats. Her eyes continued to watch me but now they were clouded with disappointment and I knew that she no longer intended to speak.

So as I drew alongside her I leaned toward her and said, "Did you have something you wanted to ask me?"

She hesitated and then shook her head. "No. Something I wanted to tell you."

I motioned her to join me. "If you've time you can tell me while I go upstairs to pick up my coat from my office. I have to drive over to the Center in New Jersey."

She nodded. A place was made for her and she followed me. Eventually the others went on their way and she and I took the elevator to the fourth floor.

It wasn't difficult to guess that she was ordinarily a shy one but she was so eager to say what she had to say that it burst from her lips, without any urging from me.

"Mr. Pace, my name's Patricia Hardisty," she blurted. (I change names and descriptions throughout the book where it's necessary to protect students' privacy — counselors, like lawyers and physicians, must safeguard confidences.) "People call me Pat," she went on, "but that's neither here nor there. What I want is to tell you the wonderful thing that's happened to me. At first I was almost afraid to believe it could be true but now I know it is. It's been long enough so it couldn't just be a coincidence or some momentary fluke. My upper back . . . I should say my shoulders. I've had constant pain in them for more than five years. Agonizing pain. So bad I could hardly do anything, work, type — I'm a writer — sit or even walk much. Whatever I did would bring on the terrible ache and pain which always got worse as the day wore on until by evening — well, I'd usually end up in tears. Actually, sometimes I'd wake up in the middle of the night because I had been sobbing in my sleep. That's how much it hurt.

"And then, about a year ago, you told that story about your friend. Remember? The one who was born into mourning?"

"Jacques," I said.

"Yes, that's the one. Jacques."

The story of Jacques — he is an American but of French stock — is one of my favorites because it's a classic example of how the study of Science of Mind can change the attitudes of a lifetime, thus resulting in a total change in the pattern of one's experience.

Jacques is a beautiful actor and I'm sure that many of you who are reading this book have seen him in a Broadway play or on TV. I first met him when I too was working in the theatre. At the time I was directing him in a play and during the breaks he and I would talk. Gradually we became friends. Later I directed him in another play. The rehearsals

13

of this one often went badly and there were days when it seemed as if everyone in the cast was at the point of hysteria.

One afternoon after we'd all been having a particularly bad time of it, Jacques dropped into a chair beside me and asked, "How do you manage to keep so calm and considerate of everybody's feelings, the way things are going? Anybody else would be screaming and climbing up the wall."

I was busy trying to figure out how to improve one of the scenes so all I could answer was, "It's the way I think."

About two weeks later my phone rang in the wee hours of the morning. I had been fast asleep and as I groggily made my way to it I found myself a little apprehensive. Who could it be at that hour? Was it bad news?

I recognized Jacques's voice immediately. He still calls me Gian which is my first name, although I've used my middle name of Eric for a number of years now.

"Gian?"

"Yes, Jacques. What's up? Something wrong?"

"Something's wrong all right. Gian, what did you mean when you said that the reason you can keep calm and all that is because of the way you think?"

It took me a moment to recall. "Oh, didn't I ever tell you that I'm a student and teacher of a discipline called Science of Mind?"

"Science of Mind? What's that?"

"Jacques, not this time of night! I was asleep and I'm bushed."

"Gian, it's important. I'm in an awful state. I'm so depressed I'm afraid of what I might do to myself. And I'll never be able to continue in the play unless I can pull myself out of it. Please, Gian."

I knew Jacques was moody and had a history of periodic and severe depressions but he'd never had one while I'd known him. I tried to think what to do.

"Look, Jacques, I'll meet you for coffee half an hour early tomorrow and tell you everything I can in that time. Later you can come and hear me lecture."

"Gian, I have to see you now. Tomorrow won't do. Please."

I sighed. "All right, Jacques, come on over."

He came and we talked half the night.

At one point I said, "Jacques, even when you're happy you have a look of sadness about you. What are you so sad about? Do you know?"

He pondered my question and then shrugged. "No. I guess I've had a feeling of sadness ever since I was a kid. Ever since I can remember."

"Sometimes, Jacques, it's . . . ." I fumbled for the right words. "Sometimes it almost seems that there's an undercurrent of perpetual mourning in you."

I saw his eyes suddenly widen and then he bent toward me and seized me by the arms. "My God, Gian, you've hit it! I was born into mourning."

"Born into mourning?"

"Yes. My father died two months before I was born. I had two aunts, his sisters, and from the time I can remember the only way they and my mother used to refer to me was as 'poor baby, poor fatherless baby.'

"And I was born at home, you know. Out in the country. One of my aunts delivered me. Can you imagine the scene, Gian? Those two fat aunts in black, mourning their brother. And my mother, probably also in black or at least covered with a black sheet. Do they have black sheets? Anyway, then I come into the world and the three of them start crying and moaning and groaning about how sad it all was and what a poor, poor fatherless baby I was.

"My God, Gian, that's what it is. I was literally born into mourning."

He threw back his handsome head and laughed. "Well, that's solved," he said. "I've had my last depression."

Actually, it wasn't quite that simple. But he began to come to my lectures and he took up the study of Science of Mind in earnest and eventually his deep, recurring depressions did become a thing of the past. Nowadays he's a pretty stable actor who never misses a performance or a TV assignment, at least not because he's in the grip of an uncontrollable depression.

The highlights of Jacques's story, of course, flashed through my mind in a matter of seconds as Patricia Hardisty and I moved toward my office, giving me time to wonder what connection that story could possibly have with the ache and pain in her shoulders or the wonderful thing that had happened to her.

And then she was telling me. "When you repeated his words, 'I was born into mourning' — I don't know — you're never going to believe this, Mr. Pace, it's so incredible — something inside me suddenly said, And what were you born into, Pat? Not mourning. New England Puritanism. The Protestant Ethic. Hard work. Plain living. No fun. Nose to the grindstone. Perfectionism. Conscientiousness. Burdens. Burdens, Mr. Pace. That's what I was born into, I kept thinking. Born into an atmosphere of shouldering burdens.

"And then as I sat there and you continued lecturing, suddenly the agonizing pain was gone from my shoulders. I couldn't believe it. I held my breath. I waited for it to return but it didn't. Not all that day. Not all that day."

She was breathless with excitement and I wanted to touch her hand to let her know I understood.

"Oh, it did return a day or so later but then I knew what to do about it. I knew that if I studied and applied what you were teaching I could sometime make it go away.

"And that's what I did, Mr. Pace. I kept studying and applying the technique and I forced myself to relax. To stop being so much of a perfectionist. To let up on work. To take time out to have fun once in a while. And most of all to quit shouldering burdens, my own and everybody else's. And it's been four months, Mr. Pace, since I've had the slightest ache or pain in my shoulders. After five years of almost being a cripple."

"That's great," I said and I felt almost as happy about it as she did. "That's just great."

"And you can bet your life, Mr. Pace, that any burdens I ever shoulder from now on will be physical ones, not mental. Burdens I can take off and lay down when they begin to give me an ache or pain across my shoulders."

I laughed and she laughed too and then as she turned to leave she added in a tone of joyous amazement, "It works, Mr. Pace. It really, really works. This stuff you're teaching."

It works, all right. "This stuff" called Science of Mind. I have no doubt about it. I've seen it work, over and over again through the years. I know what it did and is still doing for me. I know what it has done and is still doing for others. And I know what it can do for you too, if you'll learn its principles and apply its technique.

If I weren't convinced that it works I wouldn't be dedicating my life to interpreting it, explaining it and lecturing about it. I wouldn't have given up the theatre after years of training to tell others how it can help them as it's helped me. I wouldn't be writing this book to tell you how it can help you.

Let's take a specific set of problems in the area of relationships: Are you lonely? Would you like to make friends? Or are you looking for one special person? Someone to love? Do you want to get married?

Miriam wanted to get married. So she used the technique, found the right man for her and a few weeks ago they were married.

The technique of Science of Mind is just as effective in bringing together two people who belong together as it is in any other field. And giving oneself a treatment for love and marriage is as natural as giving oneself a treatment for health, prosperity or any other human concern.

I always find myself smiling when I think of Miriam, because of the amusing way she met the man who's now her husband. I'm always impressing on my students that you meet people to marry in normal ways. You don't meet them on the subway or in a singles' bar. Not that I have anything against subways or singles' bars. I've been in both often.

But those kind of struck-up acquaintanceships almost never develop into anything permanent. Or so I've always believed.

Miriam first came to one of my classes through a friend of mine, Connie. I knew her only by sight the afternoon she stopped me as I was leaving the lecture platform.

She came right to the point. She must have sensed I was in a hurry. I had an appointment for which I was already late.

"I'm getting married," she said. "And it all happened because I've been applying the things you teach. He's just what I hoped for. I met him . . . ."

I had to interrupt her and excuse myself. "Next week. I'd like to hear about it. I can't now. I haven't a minute. Next week?"

"Sure."

But I didn't have to wait until next week. The following day Connie phoned me.

"Eric?"

"Hi, Connie."

"Did my friend Miriam speak to you? Did she tell you she's getting married and how she met the man?"

"Miriam? Oh, yes, Miriam. Yes. She told me she's getting married but not how she met the man. I didn't have time to listen. I asked her to wait until next week."

"It wasn't one of your normal ways," Connie teased gleefully. "She was in an auto accident. She wasn't hurt but her car got smashed and wouldn't start and she was standing beside it, not knowing what to do. On the West Side Highway, no less. And then a car behind her stopped and a man got out, walked up to her and asked if he could help. And — you'll never guess!"

I didn't even try. "Okay, Connie. Give."

"He turned out to be a policeman. In plain clothes. On his way to a party. Only he didn't get to the party. He helped Miriam move her car off the highway and then he took her home. He also made a date for the next night. They've been going together ever since and now they're getting married. You and your struck-up acquaintances. Anyhow, Miriam says she'd been giving herself a treatment for just the kind of guy he is. For months."

What Miriam felt she needed for fulfillment was love and marriage.

Alvira's lack was of a different kind. She had an urgent necessity for money. When she learned to apply the technique she not only earned what she required but far more than she had ever expected to have in her life. Let me tell you about Alvira; she's an object lesson in achieving prosperity.

CHAPTER III

Use It for Prosperity,

Harmony, Self-Expression

Alvira came into the bookstore at the Closter, New Jersey, Science of Mind Center one day when it was fairly new. I direct that Center and I also lecture there as I do at the headquarters in New York City.

I happened to be in the bookstore when Alvira entered, having dropped in on my way to my office to chat with Mary Jane Buhler who was on substitute duty for the afternoon, but I doubt I'd have paid much attention to Alvira except for her excessive thinness and the look of despair in her large, brown eyes.

She wandered around the room, glancing at the book titles. Not touching any of the books themselves. Not taking any of them from the table or the shelves. As if she didn't quite dare or for some reason had no right.

Mary Jane and I went on talking and then suddenly Alvira was beside me, interrupting, "You're Mr. Pace, aren't you?"

"Yes."

She nodded and I realized that she had known who I was all along. "I came to hear you at last Friday's noon meeting."

Her hands had begun to tremble. She was plainly very nervous.

I encouraged her with a smile.

"I wanted to ask you a question. At the lecture. But I was scared."

I had a bit of time and obviously she could use some of it. "Why don't you ask it now?" I suggested.

"I know this isn't the way it's done." She faltered, flushing. "Barging up and interrupting you like this. But I'm desperate."

Wanting to give her privacy to talk I led her toward the door and the auditorium.

"Can I — I mean, can anyone use this teaching to make money?" she demanded softly when we were out of earshot.

"I know a great many people who have," I answered, "including myself."

She squeezed her eyes shut and begged urgently, "Tell me how. I've got to know how."

"How much do you know about the teaching?"

She opened those large, haunted eyes. "Not much. A friend told me a little about what it had done for him. And then, what I heard you say last Friday."

"Well . . . ."

"If it really works like my friend says it does I want to learn everything there is to know quick. If it can really be used for all the things he says and even to make money I need to learn it fast. If I could — if I had the money I'd buy a copy of every book in the bookstore. Read them all at one sitting. Because I'm broke. Oh, I have a job. At least I do now. But I owe a big doctor's bill and I've got to have some extra cash right away. It's desperately important. And when I say right away I mean this week."

"Wait a minute." I held up my hand. "It doesn't work quite that way. Not that it can't. But usually it doesn't. For most people it takes time to understand and absorb and convince themselves. And to practice. Come to more of the lectures. Get a book. One or two will do to start. Read them thoroughly. Apply what you read. Apply the technique. Keep at it. And if what you want is money, you'll get it."

I left her, walked back into the bookstore, picked up the first book I thought might help her and returned to where she was standing. "This is a good one," I told her. "Buy this one and study it."

She stared down at it and then raised her eyes to my face. She didn't say anything but suddenly I knew she couldn't buy that book or any other. She simply didn't have the money.

I've given books to friends, even acquaintances, but I don't recall ever having given a book to a total stranger before and I can't explain the impulse that moved me to do just that for the thin, pale girl. "Look," I said, "take this one. You don't have to buy it. I happen to have two copies in my office. I'll return one to the book table, to replace this."

She backed away from me. "Oh, no, I can't. I can't pay for it. I don't have any money. I really don't. None at all. I've got to walk home. Miles. And I had to walk to get here."

"You don't have to pay for it. I'm giving it to you."

"Please, no. I can't let you."

"I see you really don't know much about the theory I'm teaching. Listen. Listen carefully. Don't you ever again say you don't have money. Ever again. I'm sure you're familiar with the expression that the rich get richer and the poor get poorer. Now, if that's true and it seems to be, why do you suppose it happens that way?"

She shook her head doubtfully.

"To my way of thinking it's because money isn't a thing. Having money isn't having a thing. Having money is having a certain state of consciousness that produces or brings in or attracts money to us.

"The rich get richer because they have money and having money they think in terms of always having it. They assume that more will come to them as it has in the past and so it does.

"People who don't have money dwell on the fact that

they don't have it and they assume that because they haven't got it in the present they're not going to have it in the future. They're emphasizing a poverty pattern in their consciousness. And so they're going to keep on being poor."

She was gazing at me intently but a trifle dazedly.

"I'm throwing it to you all at once but if you study this book, you'll understand. I'm talking about a natural law. It has nothing to do with luck, favoritism or punishment. A person who can conceive of money coming freely to him and in ample amounts is going to have it coming freely to him and in ample amounts and then he's going to be reconvinced that he's the type of person who has money.

"But a person who is always thinking about how little money he has, who is always worrying about not having any or not having enough is never going to attract any or at least enough. And then he's going to be reconvinced that he's the type of person who never has money, who is always going to be poor, who's never going to know anything except poverty."

"I think—yes, I think I see. Kind of, anyway."

"It takes time. That's what I was trying to tell you in the beginning. But if you keep mulling it over in your thoughts . . . . Look, there's a saying attributed, I believe, to the late Mike Todd," I continued and was about to go on and tell it to her when I realized that she was so young she might not know who Mike Todd was so I backtracked to explain, "He was a famous stage and movie director and producer."

"I've heard his name," she assured me.

"Well, Mike is supposed to have once said, 'I've often been broke but I've never been poor. Poverty is a state of mind.'"

A faint smile touched her lips. She was a bright girl.

"You say you have a job but that you need extra money. Okay. Then the thing for you to do is to change your whole way of thinking about money. Don't think of it as being hard to come by. Don't think of it as coming only from your job. Think of it as being able to come to you from all sorts of un-

expected sources because you need it and believe that you're
going to get it. Here, take this book."

I thrust it into her hands.

She nearly dropped it but then she grabbed at it and
hung on.

"Now," I stressed, "you do have money. And from an
unexpected source. Since money's just a form of exchange,
in this book you have two dollars more than you had when
you came here. You've already begun to make money and
if you see it that way, you can prosper from now on."

And she has prospered. She's paid her doctor's bill and
the "extra" money she spoke of needing she must have gotten
because those big, brown eyes have a shine in them now
that's good to see. She's no longer thin and pale. She wears
beautiful clothes. All in all she's a pleasure for me to catch
sight of whenever she finds time to make it to a lecture.

And I have an idea that she's bought a copy of every
book and pamphlet in the bookstore, just as she once wanted
to do.

Alvira's case illustrates an interesting point I have recently begun to observe. People are learning to apply the
technique in all areas of life, more and more — as of course
they should. When I first began to teach, however, most of
my students seemed primarily interested in health problems.

Of course, health is still one of the big areas of concern
for a lot of people. I have men and women under medical
treatment — which we never discourage — who come to me
for help in dealing with all manner of disease, from cancer
to the common cold. Many of them have assisted in their
cure. I mean by that that they were able to use the technique
to help their physicians bring about a faster recovery than
would be considered normal in cases similar to theirs. And
I know students — Fern Parsons is one — who, without help
from me or anybody else, have, on their own, using the technique they've learned, cured themselves of just about every
illness man is heir to.

Fern is a bright, very pretty black girl who usually sits

in the front row of the auditorium when she comes to one of my evening classes. At an intermission a few weeks ago she rushed up to me to tell me she'd just gotten her voice back.

"Laryngitis," she explained. "I went to my doctor this afternoon and he said it would probably take a week or more for me to get rid of it. I couldn't even speak to him. All I could do was croak. I had to write on a· pad so he would understand."

She was talking to me in a voice that had no trace of hoarseness.

"How's that for a demonstration!" she exulted.

Science of Mind·has a few, more or less technical words in its teaching, words that are used like shorthand symbols. One word will serve for a number of words but everyone who knows it readily understands its meaning. All disciplines, like mathematics, economics, psychology, astronomy, have similar words which become part of their vocabulary.

A "demonstration" is simply a definite, satisfactory end-result or solution to whatever problem, situation or condition has been disturbing a person. In other words, the disturbing problem has been solved; the situation has disappeared; or the condition is gone or has been alleviated.

To get over a very bad case of laryngitis in a few hours is certainly a demonstration. To my mind as it was to Fern's.

"At first I couldn't figure out why," she continued. "Why I.got the laryngitis, I mean. I kept going over all the reasons that might have caused it. I discarded the obvious ones, of course. The ones I once would have blamed for causing it."

She was so excited she fairly danced along beside me. "You know, the silly beliefs that people have been accepting for generations. Like I caught cold because colds are going around. Or it happened because I was overtired. Or because I'd been sitting in a draft. Sure, colds are going around and I am tired and I suppose I have sat in a draft at some time or other lately. I'm handling a big office party my boss is giving for a dude who's retiring."

We skirted a group who were laughing and chatting.

"But I've learned to ignore those reasons. I've learned to dig deeper. Well, I kept digging. All day. And I kept using the technique. No results. I was still sick. I still couldn't talk.

"And then, right while you were lecturing — about five minutes ago — for no reason I can see, it came to me. I was angry. Really angry. Deep down angry. At my boss. I was so mad at him for piling so much work on me and for the way he keeps expecting it to be done the day before he gives it to me — well, if I could have talked I'd have blasted him. If I could have talked I'd have blasted him so loud I'd probably have ended up losing my job. And I like my job. And my boss. Most of the time.

"Wow! Right away when I thought of it, I knew that was it. I lost my voice so I wouldn't lose my job. I also knew I'd have my voice back when I tried to speak. And I have. Just listen. Wow, what about that?"

"That," I answered, pleased, "is a capital 'd' Demonstration."

"It sure is," she agreed. "It sure is."

She moved on just as a long arm and big hand appeared, to grasp my shoulder. "Hi, there, swinger. How's it going, Eric, my friend?"

Ward Edwards. He too had once had a health problem, far more serious than Fern's, but he'd completely overcome it.

Ward is a huge man, strong, with a barrel-like chest. His skin is fair. His hair is reddish blond. His eyes are a vivid blue and the first time I met him they were stormy with years of pent-up hate and anger and bitterness — and more than a scrap of self-pity.

I had never seen him before the blisteringly hot summer day several years earlier, when he arrived at my office. He had made the appointment, he informed me bluntly and a bit rudely, only because I was a last resort. He had tried everything else, including psychiatry. Actually he didn't really expect I could help.

His manner was rough and his speech not always correct but I soon discovered that he was very intelligent, self-taught and well-read.

I asked him what his trouble was and he lost no time in telling me. Nothing was right in his world. At least as far as he was concerned. He hated his job. He hated his boss. All the women he knew were out to get their hooks in him and not one of them was worth a tinker's damn. His health was terrible. He had high blood pressure. He'd been under care for it over a year but his physician despaired of the way he was responding to treatment. His back bothered him every waking moment. He did have a few bucks in the bank but doctor bills were slowly eating them away.

When he'd finished the recital of his present woes he glared at me and added, "Before you go into your song and dance about how all I got to do is learn a few principles and practice a technique and everything is going to come up roses, I'd also like to fill you in on a few more facts. About my childhood this time."

I didn't respond to his obvious antagonism. I waited to find out if he'd come to see me for any other reason than to attack me.

"I wasn't even an orphan, see," he continued. "If I hadda been what happened to me might be easier to understand. But I had live parents like everybody else. Could still have live ones for all I know. Only my old man took off when I was two years old. For parts unknown, as they say. And I never heard nothing from him since, except once. Yeah, once. When I got the Purple Heart and the story was in all the papers. Weeks after a letter reached me from some place in Mexico and in it was a clipping of the story and a picture of me he must have cut out from some newspaper or other and with them was a note. It had just nine words in it: 'I tell them all you're my son. Your dad.'

"Nine words, mind you. After all those years. And his son! He hadn't remembered that when he took off, had he?"

I tried to say something but he silenced me with a wave.

"Oh, there's more," he declared. "A lot more. You haven't heard the part about my mother and the foster home where I ended up at three when she took off too, with another man. I have an older sister. Have or had. I don't know which. Two years older.

"Well, the old lady — my mother — she took my sister with her but she left me with a neighbor. She didn't bother to tell the neighbor she was high tailing it for good and when she didn't return I got sent off to this God-forsaken place in Maine. Way the hell away from everything. Near the Canadian border. It was run by two sisters. The younger sister had three children of her own, two girls and a boy."

The clanging of a fire engine racing down Fifth Avenue came shatteringly through the open window of my office. We were having trouble with the building's air-conditioning and the heat in the room was oppressive. I looked at him questioningly. "The noise . . . . Would you like me to close the window? The air-conditioning's not working and I'm afraid we'll be even more uncomfortable."

"Do as you like," he answered. "I don't care one way or the other."

And he took up the thread where he'd left off. "The boy was eight years older than me. And he hated me from the start. There were four other kids there in the same boat as me. Foster kids, I mean. But they were all females. And he'd been the only boy until I came along. I don't know what difference it made to him. I was really no more than a baby but he figured me some kind of a threat, I guess. Why I'll never know. Because those two dames — his mother and her sister — they battered me around like they did the others. They didn't favor me none.

"And when I say battered, I mean battered. They'd think nothing of giving us a series of blows across the face if we talked too much or laughed or got excited over something. Not that there was ever much to laugh or get excited about. Except maybe a new calf.

"Birthdays? Forget it. I never knew I had one. Or that

anybody else did, for that matter. Ice cream? I had my first taste of that delicacy when I was fourteen and the authorities took me to a nearby city to testify against them — the two sisters. 'For their brutality to children' were the words that they used. Yeah, the authorities had finally found them out. Which saved a few other kids from getting banged around and terrorized but didn't help me none. I'd already gotten the beating that twisted my spine and left me with this bad back I got."

"Look, Mr. Edwards, I . . . ."

"Yeah, this bad back of mine. I got it from a beating. Can you believe that? A real beating. With four strands of rope." He paused to glare at me again and then ordered, "Now let me hear you tell me how I can change all that by just changing the state of my thoughts."

I'm not in the field of psychiatry and by that time I wasn't sure he really wanted any part of the sort of help I could give him. I understood by then why he was so angry and bitter and full of self-pity and I deeply sympathized with him but I knew my understanding and sympathy weren't going to change anything for him unless we could indeed change the state of his thoughts. But I also felt I ought to let him get it all out first. "One of those women actually beat you until your spine was injured?" I asked. "With a rope?"

"One of the women? Hell, no. Not that time. Oliver. The son. He was sixteen. I was eight. He took me out to the barn one day and beat me until I was unconscious. I ain't never been able to comprehend what for. I ain't sure his reason was even clear to him. He just felt like beating somebody and I was there.

"And then he tossed me into a corner of the barn and left me. I didn't come to until his mother found me the next morning and she was kind enough to give me a couple of clouts on the head and shoulders for staying out all night and for fighting with Oliver. A real motherly type, huh?"

"Incredible," I answered.

"That's putting it mildly," he said. "And it's all true.

Every word. I swear it. Well, that about does it. That was the low spot in my life. Anything else I could tell you couldn't compare with it. Not for downright misery."

He leaned back in the chair and his barrel-round chest heaved. "Like I said, let's hear you tell me how I can change all that by just changing my thoughts," he challenged again.

I decided to tackle him head-on. "I'm going to have to put a direct question to you. I can't help you if you don't really want my help. Do you? Or did you just come here to tell me that you don't believe what I'm teaching?"

Like many people who are openly belligerent he didn't have strong defenses. I could see them crumble as he shifted his eyes. One thing that makes me happy is to have people drop their defenses with me because it indicates that I've created an atmosphere in which another human being can dare to abandon his ego protections and let his creative self come through.

He opened his mouth, closed it again. I too remained silent. He had to make the choice.

When at last he did speak he sounded much less hostile. "Yes," he admitted, "you're right. I suppose you could say that that's precisely what I came for. To tell you I don't believe what you teach. Anyone who listens to you and believes what you say — he'd have to believe he could get rid of a past like mine like it never existed. Now that just ain't logical to me. It's always going to be there and it's always going to hurt."

"Yes, it's always going to be there in fact," I agreed. "As a past experience. Our past is always going to be there in fact for all of us. None of us can change that. We all have to learn to live with that reality. But no, you're wrong that it always has to hurt and affect our present. It only affects our present if we keep dwelling on it, regretting it, feeling bitter about it or sorry for ourselves because of it. Sometimes I think self-pity is the most destructive emotion of all. These are the attitudes that keep the past alive, haunting us, bothering us, preventing us from moving forward. If we change the way we think and feel about it we can get rid of its hurt and bondage. And we can get rid of the pain situations it still causes in our life today."

He wasn't convinced but he was no longer fighting me. "Pain situations," he repeated thoughtfully. "I like that. It aptly describes them."

Our talk that day ran well over half an hour. He wasn't greatly changed when he left my office but he didn't drop out of class and as the weeks went by I noticed that he looked less and less angry and bitter. Six months later he made another appointment to see me and we began working on his problems in earnest. We soon discovered he had a pattern of always getting fired from jobs or quitting because he lacked a basic feeling of self-worth. Which, of course, wasn't surprising with his background. And we also discovered a couple of other things that were surprising. One was that his high blood pressure, which hadn't responded to medical treatment, was caused by his extreme anger over the things that had been done to him as a child, since as his anger decreased his blood pressure dropped, slowly becoming normal. Another was that his hostility toward women actually masked a fear that no woman could love him because the only women he had known in his childhood had neither loved him nor treated him kindly.

Today he is happily married. He's been at the same job going on two years and shows every sign of liking it and planning to remain in it. He's fond of his boss and I'll bet his boss is fond of him. His health is excellent. His past is dead in his emotions. His present and future are very much alive

Neal, Miriam, Alvira, Fern, Ward and Patricia Hardisty — each felt that something was wrong or lacking in his or her life. Each wanted something — health, marriage, money, freedom from a difficult situation in the present or from the hurts and pains of an unfortunate past. Each got what he or she wanted.

What do you feel is wrong with your life? What do you feel is lacking?

CHAPTER IV

To Change Your Experience,

Change Your Consciousness

I've told you that what this teaching called Science of Mind has done for me and for others it can do for you. And by now you may be thinking impatiently, Let's get on with it. Just what is this teaching? What are these principles? What is this technique you're talking about? How do I learn to apply it?

At this stage I feel it's safe to assume that you wouldn't be reading this book if you didn't have problems and weren't looking for solutions to those problems. Or if you weren't dissatisfied with what you've done or are doing with your talents and abilities — with your life.

In my personal search through the various disciplines to find meaning and purpose in my own experience I gained many valuable insights. But each time I reached a point where I could go no further. Something was missing.

What good, I would ask myself, baffled and confused, were insights if I didn't know how to put them to use and effect changes in those areas of my world where I wanted change? What good was just theorizing?

What was needed, I realized, was a method, a technique,

by which I could take the knowledge I was learning about myself and employ it to improve the state of my affairs. And not only to be able to employ it sometimes but to be able to employ it at all times, in all places and under all circumstances, decisively, actively and consistently.

Of course I was aware that what I was asking for was a pretty tall order because techniques in the field of self-improvement are always cropping up and like a lot of other people I'd tried a number of them. But invariably my enthusiasm had waned as the results achieved in each case fell short of my expectation.

Almost from the moment, however, that the technique of Science of Mind was explained to me I believe I knew that it was going to be something I could use for a lifetime, that as my application and understanding of it increased, its effectiveness would increase. The principles behind it made perfect sense to me. I could accept them on both an emotional and an intellectual level.

Occasionally a beginner in one of my classes will ask, "But isn't this technique really just auto-suggestion?"

My answer is, No, it is not auto-suggestion. Auto-suggestion depends on the power of the human mind to achieve its results. The technique of Science of Mind is not thus limited; to achieve its results it utilizes the creative power of the universe, the Infinite Intelligence behind all things.

But to utilize anything one must understand it, what it is, why it works, how it works.

In the beginning I said that anyone can understand the principles and learn to apply the technique and I am convinced that anyone can.

So I am first going to state each principle as simply as I can and then I'm going to go into it in more detail and eventually I'm going to discuss its importance in the teaching as a whole. I know that no one is going to spend much time applying a technique if he or she isn't persuaded of the truth of the principles on which the technique rests. I certainly wouldn't.

A few years ago I moved into a new (for me) apartment in midtown Manhattan. Because of my work in counseling I have to have a telephone. That was the first item on my priority list. I phoned the utility company from the place of a friend of mine and told them why I had to have a phone installed forthwith if not sooner. They promised to have a man at my apartment in the morning.

And sure enough, one was. Bright and early. Or at least it semed bright and early to me. I'd had to get out of bed to let him in, having been up late the night before, unpacking, arranging and rearranging furniture, trying to induce the living room to look like home.

Well, to make a long story short, the man arrived bright and early and he spent the better part of the day in my apartment. Now this was a mechanic who was supposed to know how to install a telephone. At least he was sent by the phone company. Anyway, after studying the problem from every conceivable angle, going out, coming back in, going out again, coming back in again, in, out, up, down, much pondering, he finally informed me, "It's impossible to put a telephone in this apartment."

I stared at him in amazement. "How can it be impossible to put a telephone in a New York apartment? In the heart of a city?"

I was very polite. I refrained from citing the statistics I'd recently read in an almanac that showed that 98 per cent of New York homes have telephones, that over 90 per cent of the farm homes in the state have phones.

Or maybe it wasn't politeness. Maybe I sensed the futility of arguing with him. His was obviously not an open mind.

"That's the way it is," he insisted loftily. "The nearest hook-up box is — (he mentioned an address a block away). It's just impossible to install a phone at this location."

And off he went.

I double-quicked it over to my friend's and phoned the telephone company.

Within three quarters of an hour another man was at my door. He was a supervisor, no less, and I can't say for sure but I have a suspicion that he'd had his pre-dinner cocktail before breakfast and his nightcap before lunch.

After removing his hat and coat he went through a shorter version of the same routine as the first man and at the end he agreed with the mechanic. He actually did. He agreed that it was impossible to put a telephone in my apartment.

For the second time that day I ran to my friend's and phoned the telephone company. And this time I let them have it. I all but threatened to write my congressman. I told them they were a public service company, supposed to provide service to the citizens of New York and that I was a citizen and that my work involved emergency calls and that something had to be done immediately.

They promised me they would send another man bright and early the next morning.

Bright and early the next morning I opened my door to a jaunty little man who broke off whistling to give me a happy-go-lucky grin. "What seems to be the trouble?" he asked.

I told him my long, sad tale.

"I can't see any problem," he said. "We've just got to connect you up to the junction box that's designated in the records as — (he gave the same address as the other two men)."

"But that's what the other men said and that address is a whole block away," I explained, feeling as if I were smack in the middle of a recurring nightmare.

"Oh, no," he assured me. "It just happens to have that address as its designation. It's probably right down in your basement. Do you know how to get to the basement?"

I nodded. "Sure. You press the elevator button marked 'B' I'll come with you."

So the jaunty little man and I went out to the elevator, got in and pressed the button marked 'B' and within a few seconds we were in the basement. Stepping out he walked over to an enormous black box. Nobody could have missed it.

"Here it is," he announced. And then, "But there is one difficulty. I'm going to have to run the line through that alleyway out there and up the back wall to your kitchen window. And the thing is I'm going to have to bore a hole in your window frame. In order to get the wire through."

"I don't care," I said. "Be my guest. Bore two holes. I'll plug one up. Anything. Just get the phone in."

He began whistling again. I left him and went upstairs and in less than an hour and a half he had a working telephone with a bedroom extension installed in my apartment.

This encounter with the telephone men emphasized for me that in order to make a technique work, one has to understand the principles behind it. Not some of the principles but all of the principles. The two men who couldn't connect up my telephone with the company's network thought the designation of a junction box defined its location. The jaunty little man who made the connection knew that it didn't. So he was the one who got results.

Science of Mind is based not only on the most recent findings of science and philosophy about the origins of things, the things themselves and the way they work—about cause in the universe we know—it is also, in the words of the American philosopher Ernest Holmes, its original expositor, "a result of the best thought of the ages."

One of the most important premises of the teaching is that whether you are healthy or sick, whether you are happy or unhappy, whether you are poor or prosperous, whether you are lonely or surrounded by friends and loved ones, whether you are successful or a failure, depends in great measure on how you use your mind. The principles explain why this is so and why, if you want to change your experience, you must learn to direct your mind. And the technique gives you an easy, practical method by which you can direct it, by which you can gain the necessary mastery over your thoughts and emotions.

To Change Your Experience, Change Your Consciousness

The principles are easy to grasp:
1) There is one creative Power in the universe, whatever one chooses to call It.
2) Thought — thinking and feeling — starts and carries through the creative process.
3) Thought creates form by an immutable law of cause and effect.
4) Change negative thinking to purposeful affirmative thinking and you change unpleasant experiences to desirable ones.

The first principle of Science of Mind is that there is one Power, whether It is called 'Absolute Mind' by philosophy or 'God' by religion or 'Order' by science. There are not two powers. There is only one Power. And this Power, this Universal or Absolute Mind, this Infinite Intelligence, this Original and First Cause is in all, through all, as all. It is in all, through all, as all, because It creates everything out of Itself, there being nothing else out of which It could create anything.

It is, we say, omnipotent, omnipresent, omniscient. That is, it is all powerful; it is present everywhere, at every point in time and space and on every plane of existence, not only on the dimension of this universe of which our earth is a part; and it is all-knowing, knows every person, place and thing.

And the way that this Infinite Intelligence creates is by thinking, within Itself, upon Itself, about Itself, there being no other self within which or upon which or about which for It to think. There being, in fact, nothing else anywhere but It.

This is a second principle upon which the technique is based. Thought, then, is what starts the creative process and in this case we mean by thought the thinking and feeling activities of the mind.

Now what this means to you and me — aside from an explanation of the what, how and why of the universe — is that when this Infinite Intelligence, this one Power, this Absolute Mind, evolved man as a self-conscious aspect of Itself on this earth plane It evolved him with free will, with the ability

37

to choose. And it further evolved him with the ability to create in a manner similar to the way by which It creates — by thinking.

That man creates by thinking is an idea that often strikes my students as surprising. And yet that's what they've been doing since they first began to think. The relationships they've had and are having, the experiences they've undergone and are undergoing, the conditions they've been in and are in, have largely been created by their thought. Mostly the thought has not been consciously directed and mostly it has run counter to what they'd be trying to think if they knew that their thought is what produces the forms, circumstances and events in their lives.

This brings us to a third principle which is that not only does thought produce form but it produces form by an immutable law — the creative law of cause and effect. We usually refer to it simply as the Law.

So that the concept is easier to understand I'll explain it in a number of different ways. One may make it clear where another may not.

Your mental attitude for the most part is what determines your experience. Your dominant thoughts produce whatever conditions exist in your surroundings. And that means in your body as well as in your affairs. What you are thinking and feeling most of the time inevitably becomes what you experience. Your outer world is a more or less exact copy of the inner world of your mind. The thoughts you dwell on, the images you picture, the emotions you harbor, the ideas you contemplate and meditate upon, the fantasies you fantasize, the visions you envision, the dreams you dream, already reflect or at some future time will reflect themselves as forms (conditions, situations, relationships) in your life.

Anything in form is the result of thought. Thought is cause; form is effect. What a person is and what he is experiencing is the result of the predominant state of his thought. Science of Mind expresses it thus: The Law responds by corresponding.

And when one finally comes to understand this creative law of life and the way it works, one learns to keep one's thoughts and emotions centered and focused on what one wants to experience, recognizing that to do otherwise is sheer folly.

I have said that the Law is immutable. By that I mean that it is fixed, unchangeable and no more subject to entreaties or appeals than any other law in the universe. It can be ignored, misused or not consciously used at all but it continues to work according to its nature, whatever our attitude toward it.

If your health is bad, if you feel you're an utter failure, if you don't know a person you could call a friend and if your finances are in terrible shape, you may find it hard to swallow the bitter pill that you yourself are mainly responsible, that by your thoughts and emotions you have created these conditions.

Here I would emphasize that it is important to accept this knowledge without guilt for that which has occurred in one's past but rather to accept it as a key for controlling that which occurs in one's present and will occur in one's future.

The thing to realize at this point is that form (and this includes relationships) is never permanent. Conditions can always be changed. If certain thoughts have produced certain forms, other thoughts can and will produce other forms.

Change negative thoughts to affirmative thoughts and we change negative, unpleasant experiences to affirmative, pleasant experiences.

And that's our great hope — that to change thought is to change experience. That's our second, third, fourth — our ad infinitum chance. To alter thought and emotions is to alter forms. That's our another opportunity. That's our ultimate deliverance from past bondage. That's our final freedom to chart another course along a path we'd really like to go.

Again, the basic principles of Science of Mind are, briefly:
1) There is only One Power.

2) Thought creates form.
3) The creative law of cause and effect is immutable.
4) Change your thinking and you change your experiences.

CHAPTER V

Six Steps in Mastering
the Technique

Behind the technique of Science of Mind lie several great truths.

No situation, no condition, no form is permanent. We can change any condition, any situation, any form in our life by putting another pattern of causation into our mind. We do not have to depend on our own human power to make the changes we desire. Surrounding us, within us, for our use, is the Infinite Intelligence which created the universe and which always reacts to our thoughts, not in a haphazard way but according to a law of cause and effect.

Don't fuss with results, I tell my students. Work with causes. Otherwise you are merely solving one problem to replace it with another or exchanging one symptom for another.

Let's start with a predicament many of us have gotten into at one time or another but that isn't too serious for most of us.

You get up one morning, make your way sleepily to the bathroom and step on the bathroom scale.

No!

You bend over and peer down again — hopefully. The needle can't actually have registered the number you thought it did.

But yes, it does, and you quickly step off the scale in dismay. You are five pounds heavier than you were the last time you weighed yourself and you were overweight then.

That does it, you tell yourself. No more stalling. I am going to lose weight. I've got to.

Gray day. No more sweets. No more desserts. No more second helpings. No more ice cream. And especially no more chocolate cake.

You firm your jaw. You marshal your will power. You have made your decision and you are determined to stick to it this time, come the reverse of heaven and high water.

Your will power lasts through the morning and lunch but by mid-afternoon you find yourself gobbling down a piece of chocolate cake and, moreover, with a scoop of ice cream on top.

Guiltily you look the other way and try to think up an adequate excuse for your transgression, And, naturally, you secretly hate yourself for your weakness.

Why? Why did you do it when you really didn't want to? The answer is simple. Whenever there's a battle between the will and the emotions, the emotions usually win out.

Your emotions wanted and needed that chocolate cake and ice cream, even though your intellect told you you'd be foolish to eat them, that you ought to lose weight.

I know. I sympathize. It's happened on occasion to me too. And it would appear to be a pretty hopeless situation except for one thing. Science now knows that the conscious mind (where the will is) can redirect the subconscious mind (where the emotions are).

Using this knowledge, the technique of Science of Mind teaches us how to place conscious, rational choices into the subconscious mind in order to achieve the experiences we wish.

One evening I was sitting in my office with two of my

close friends, both of whom have been in the teaching of Science of Mind nearly as long as I have. We were doing some end-of-the-day talking and trying to decide where to go for dinner. I knew I wasn't with it and hadn't been very good company or cooperative so finally I said, "Look, just ignore me. I've had a tough day and I realize I'm not in a good mood. You two make the decision and wherever you want to go, I'll just go along too."

They nodded and Vicki turned to David and asked, "How about Chinese food? I like it and I haven't had any recently."

"Good idea," David replied. "Love it myself."

"Oh, but I'd rather have spaghetti. Or something Italian," I protested.

"Be quiet," Vicki told me, "and come along. You gave up your right to choose."

She was right and shamefacedly I had to admit it and tag after them to the restaurant they selected.

That time I had to experience what they chose because I hadn't made a choice of my own but I try not to make such mistakes often. Of course it was a little thing and of no consequence but many people are giving as little conscious direction to what they experience in the important areas of their lives.

The technique of Science of Mind, let me repeat, is called treatment. Unfortunately treatment is a word that can have unpleasant connotations because of its possible association with illness, doctors and the medical profession in general. And for that reason many of us who use it frequently wish that a more satisfactory word could be found as a substitute. Occasionally "declaration" or something similar is tried as an alternative and once in awhile someone coins an entirely new expression but each has been discovered to have its own limitations.

I got around my own objection to the word a long time ago by thinking of it in terms of what a goldsmith does to a lump of gold when he wants to make some specific form or forms out of it; say, two plates and a goblet. He "treats" it by a process basically chemical. Or—he gives it "treatment." Treatment as the goldsmith uses it is simply the way he changes the gold from one form to another. Treatment as we use it is simply the way we change the patterns of thought and feeling in our mind from one state to another.

I usually teach the technique of Science of Mind treatment to beginners in six steps. The names of the steps are easy to memorize:

1) Definition
2) Identification
3) Recognition
4) Denial
5) Affirmation
6) Committal

I am first going to explain these steps and then I am going to illustrate them with a specific treatment.

The first step in treatment is definition, to define the source of the Power that makes it work. Science of Mind treatment is a process designed to create new causation. This new causation consists of different thoughts or ideas, different emotional patterns or mental pictures. It generally comprises ideas, reactions or pictures of health, love, abundance, peace, balance, success and happiness, in place of their opposites. Since a treatment is always a creative process, it is begun with a statement defining the one creative Power in the universe: Mind, God, Order, Intelligence — however you think of it. It is through knowing what the Power is and that you are It individualized that you realize that your ability to effect change is not limited by human mind capabilities as you may have thought. The Power is unlimited. It is always equal to any challenge.

How should you go about defining the Power? Anyway you want that makes sense to you. There are, of course, numerous ways and I'll be presenting examples throughout the remainder of the book.

All the synonyms of good you can think of are synonyms

for the one Power and thus since you are aligning yourself with this source of all good, it is important to try to keep expanding your understanding of It.

The thing to remember is that your definition should contain clear reminders to yourself, in meaningful terms for you, of just what the Power is and the attributes of good It possesses which are applicable to your personal problem or problems. Actually your definition need not vary much from treatment to treatment although it probably will as time goes on. As you contemplate It, you will discover more and more of Its facets and inevitably your concept of It will enlarge.

If you're having difficulty with your definition I suggest you begin with something like the following: There is one Mind, one Infinite Intelligence, one Life, one Love. And then, if your problem is health, you should add, one Health. Or if it is lack of money you could add, one Abundance or one great Infinite Supply. Use your imagination. You are convincing yourself, no one else. You are changing your consciousness and you probably instinctively know as well as anybody how to accomplish that.

The second step in treatment is identification, to identify yourself with the Power as you defined It in the first step. You state that you are some part of that Power, that you are that Power as you defined It, individualized. It is in you, through you and as you. What you are doing is realizing that the one Power is perfect, that you as that Power individualized are perfect and that therefore your experience has to be perfect.

At this point you may begin to doubt, to question, to hesitate. How do you know that the one Power is in you? How do you know that you are It, as we say in Science of Mind jargon?

Well, think about it a moment. If there's only one Universal Mind, one Infinite Intelligence, that creates everything out of Itself, then you have to be It because there is nothing else. It is what you and I are, what everybody, everything is. Your "I am" is the cosmic I AM, operating as you.

Thus, step two should be something like the following: I am that Mind, that Infinite Intelligence, that Life, that Love, that Health (or Abundance) individualized.

Or your statement could be: That Mind, that Intelligence, that Life, that Love, that Health, that Abundance is in all, through all and as all. Therefore It is in me, through me and as me.

Always bring treatment down to yourself. Make it specific for you.

The third step in treatment is recognition, to recognize the availability of good and your specific good in particular and to recognize that that good is available right here and right now.

People have a tendency to think that any good that's going to come to them is going to come to them sometime in the future. Or they may be unable to imagine themselves as the recipient of any good at all, seeing the world as hostile to them, grim and full of evil. In this step we clear our minds of patterns of thought and feeling that could doom our efforts at the start. We convince ourselves that, regardless of the conditions we're in, regardless of our circumstances, regardless of what we lack, this is a universe of good, that that good is always present, at all times and in all places, ready for the accepting.

At this point some perceptive soul is going to raise a very pertinent question, "Do you mean to tell me that the instant I recognize that my good is available then it is actually available as a material form? Do you mean to tell me that the minute I complete a treatment for — say, a car — that a Cadillac is going to materialize right in front of me or going to appear parked outside my door? You must be either a madman or a magician."

If that's what I meant I guess I'd have to be considered a madman because I'm not a magician. And none of the magicians I knew in my theatre days could have performed an act like that. No, I don't mean anything of the sort. I have emphasized and now I'll reemphasize that a treatment starts in mind and is completed in mind. When you start your treatment the result you want only exists in the world of form as a potentiality.

Let me explain a little more, as I explain in my classes. The money I'm going to handle next week, next month or even next year exists in the economy as a potentiality. It may be circulating right now and on its way to the point where it becomes mine. Or it may be just being printed down at the Bureau of Engraving in Washington. Or it may be in the form of wood and cloth and chemicals that are being made into paper. But at whatever stage it's in — if only as the seeds and ore from which the raw materials will come in the course of growing, harvesting and mining — it is there as potentiality.

You don't have to make a big deal out of this step if you don't need to. You don't have to engage in a philosophical discourse or a theological colloquy. Remember you are only convincing yourself. You may only need to say something like: My good is available right here and right now and I accept it.

A treatment is not so much a matter of words as it is a consciously-directed movement of thought.

The third step in treatment makes our minds receptive to our good and when that good is accepted in consciousness it is inevitably going to appear in the material world.

The fourth step in treatment is denial, to deny the condition, situation or relationship you want to eliminate from your experience. The denial is always brief and may be omitted if dwelling on the negative tends to establish it more firmly in your mind. However it is important not to omit the step if the negative has a strong hold on you. You may be able to make it disappear from your conscious mind if you ignore it but that is not the same thing as eliminating it. Merely repressed, it can remain in your subconscious to continue to cause you distress and unhappiness, if not in the same form then in another form equally unpleasant.

Part of this step may also be to negate and nullify the

negative state of mind or pattern of thought which is responsible for the undesirable thing you are experiencing.

As we've learned, conditions and situations usually don't just happen. They are caused and for everything that we are experiencing in our outer world there is an inner emotion, picture, thought, belief, that corresponds to it and has caused it. In Science of Mind we call these inner emotions, pictures, thoughts and beliefs "mental equivalents." Doctors who practice psychosomatic medicine search for these inner causes of distress and disease, hoping to get rid of them and thereby get rid of the disease that has resulted from harboring them.

Mental equivalents are not always easy to discover in oneself or anyone else. But we shall be discussing them again and again as we take up various problems and their solutions. Now, just to illustrate by example, I'll briefly mention several generally accepted ones.

But first I must warn you that none of them is universal in the sense that it applies in every case. They are tools or guides to help. They are not rigid formulas.

Colds — nasal and chest congestion — can often be traced to a pattern of confused thought or a feeling of hurt (over which we are "sniffling").

A limited income may stem from the unconscious belief that poverty is a virtue or from an unconscious image of oneself as poor, limited, inadequate or unworthy. It might stem from the self-fulfilling prophecy of another person and it might also stem from a guilty fear of earning more than a parent whom one ambivalently loves and hates.

A feeling of lack of self-worth can cause an automobile accident. Maybe you think this statement is far-fetched but I'm convinced that it did cause one for me. The accident did happen, it happened to me, and I traced it in my consciousness to a loss of self-esteem. In a series of events somebody had been slyly undermining my efforts to achieve a certain goal, so slyly that I had been unable to grapple with the problem openly or even to be certain that I was right in my assessment of the situation.

Thwarted, I had begun, without being fully cognizant of the fact, to doubt my ability, my worth. It was a subtle thing and it might have gone on escaping my notice except for the "accident."

On a spring afternoon I was returning from the Closter Center to my Manhattan apartment in one of my most prized possessions, a brand new, bright yellow and black hard-top convertible. I had picked it up from the dealer less than two months before, on St. Patrick's Day, and I had named it Sean Patrick in honor of the double occasion. I like to name my cars. It gives me a feeling of closeness, a feeling that we operate more smoothly together.

Anyway, Sean Patrick and I were approaching the farthest toll booth of the George Washington Bridge on the Jersey side. I hadn't been mulling over the frustrating situation I've mentioned but I suppose it had crossed my mind once or twice that day. I wasn't driving fast and I thought I was driving carefully.

But suddenly — a crash and a jolt.

I had hit the toll booth stanchion with the left front fender.

"Why not another car?" a friend of mine joked when she heard. "You might have been able to blame the other driver."

My insurance broker had even more fun at my expense. "Does the person in the toll booth wish to press charges?" he queried solemnly.

I looked him straight in the eye and tried to sound penitent at my oversight. "You know I never thought to ask? Should I have? I just backed up, straightened course and got the heck out of there. Anyway the toll booth was going too fast and it was in the wrong lane."

He laughed.

I joined him because I'd long since discovered and routed out the inner pattern of inferiority that had resulted in an outer attempt to prove I wasn't worthy of my beautiful and perfect new car.

Does that mean that if I ever again should suffer a feeling of lack of self-worth I'm going to get into another accident? Definitely not; I have taken care of that possibility by treating myself for a pattern of safe driving.

Cars and stars have at least one thing in common — the "accidents" that happen to them are never really accidental. Cosmic accidents have causes traceable to scientific laws of probability and human accidents have causes traceable to negative patterns in consciousness. Students of Science of Mind learn early to search for hidden mental causes back of the things that happen to them, apparently for no reason. Usually they uncover some pattern of thought which, if known sooner and altered, would have made it possible for them to escape or avoid the incident.

Again, finding the mental equivalent may take some digging but don't let that stop you. One thing you can always do is to use the time-proven device of declaring that whatever the pattern of thought or state of mind that has caused your trouble, you want it negated and nullified. You want it out of your mind, out of your life. At some future time, when the emotional charge has gone from the situation, the pattern will often reveal itself to you.

Thus, in step four, you might state: I deny that my income is limited (if it is) and I negate and nullify whatever pattern of thought in my subconscious mind has caused it to appear to be limited.

The fifth step in treatment is affirmation, to affirm the condition, situation or relationship you do want in your experience. You declare that you have it or that you are it. You affirm the opposite of every negative thing for which you are giving yourself the treatment.

For example, you affirm that you are or have health if you are sick. You affirm that you have plenty, abundance, prosperity and a limitless supply if your income is limited. Affirm as much good that is applicable to your problem as you can think of.

This is the step where you state what you are setting into

motion. This is the step where, if you are doing it audibly, you clearly hear what you are putting into your consciousness and can catch yourself if it involves something you don't want to experience.

Continue to make affirmations until you feel (achieve a sense of complete conviction) that the thing or things you are treating for (the good you seek, the perfection you want) are accepted in your mind and established in your consciousness. You continue to make positive, constructive statements until you have a feeling of 'Okay, I know it's done.' Or 'I have it.' Or 'Everything's fine,' 'Everything's right.'

The sixth step in treatment is committal, to commit the treatment into the Law of Mind, the creative law of cause and effect, recognizing that the Law does the work. You release the treatment into the Law; you entrust it to the Law; you leave it to the Law to do the work, knowing that the Law is automatic, that it will bring about the demonstration you want. But in its own way. You do not limit the operation of the Law by masterminding how it should operate.

Telling you to commit your treatment into the Law and then let it do the work sounds like I'm telling you to do your treatment and then sit back, wait and do nothing. But that is emphatically not what I'm telling you to do. Yes, you must commit your treatment to the Law and know that it does the work, not you, but you must later take the action which is presented to you (which results from the treatment).

I can't be too definite about this: Treatment that does not result in action is mental evasion. The Power, the Mind, the Intelligence can't do anything for you that it doesn't do through you. You can't treat for a new apartment with a beautiful view and then sit in your room and do nothing about finding that apartment. The Law will lead you to the right apartment for you but you have to let it lead you, by taking a logical action that could result in finding an apartment.

Or you can't do, as a girl I know did who was treating herself for a job. You can't treat for a job and then make no effort to make yourself employable.

"I've been treating every day for a couple of months," she told me, "and somebody else always gets the jobs I go after."

I know her well enough to give it to her straight, "Well, if you've been doing a treatment for a job every day, you haven't been listening to it. You haven't been taking the action that would help you get a job."

"Yes, I have," she insisted. "I've applied at five different places."

"Looking the way you do now, your make-up not on straight, your hair uncombed and the hem of your dress stapled?" I asked.

She had the grace to blush. "The hem got caught and I didn't have time to sew it."

"Take time," I advised. "Anyone appraising you for a job is very probably going to assume that the way you 'do' yourself is the way you're going to do the job and they may not bother to try to find out whether or not they're right."

She wasn't happy with my candor but she took my advice and eventually did get the job she was looking for.

To repeat a word of caution — if you don't release your treatment into the Law consciously, you begin to think you have to make it happen and then you limit the results to your own human mind reasoning. You don't make it happen; you just take the action that is presented to you.

And a suggestion — it is always advisable, whenever you can achieve privacy, to speak your treatments aloud. There are two reasons for this. Hearing the words doubly impresses them on your consciousness. And people tend to organize their thoughts better, to think more concretely and to find it easier to keep their minds from straying from the matter at hand when they are speaking than when they are thinking silently.

At this point I think it would be appropriate to summarize the technique of treatment. Try to discover by introspection, rumination, or a flash of intuitive insight the inner emotion, picture, thought or belief — the mental equivalent —

responsible for your problem. If you can't, deal with the cause in general terms; tell yourself that whatever the cause is, you negate it. Then:

1) Define the source of the Power that is all.
2) Identify yourself with the Power as you defined It.
3) Recognize that the specific good you want is available right here and right now and accept it.
4) Deny the condition, situation or relationship you want to eliminate from your experience and negate and nullify the negative state of mind or pattern of thought that produced its temporary appearance.
5) Affirm the condition, situation or relationship you want in your experience; declare that you have it or that you are it; affirm the opposite of every negative you are nullifying.
6) Commit the treatment to the creative law of cause and effect recognizing that the Law produces the manifestation as you take the action that it presents to you.

CHAPTER VI

Magnetizing What You Want

in Life

Using all the parts of treatment I am now going to give a specific treatment as an example of the process. A good idea, I think, would be to take the case of the would-be dieter who has not been able to resist the chocolate cake and ice cream. Putting all the steps together I'll form a specific treatment that will help that beleaguered one to lose weight and acquire a slim, trim figure, provided he or she practices applying it.

First, of course, as our hypothetical specimen himself or herself should do, I'll try to find out what kind of negative thinking produced the problem in the beginning.

Anyone who is overweight should try to find out the causes — or, as we call them, the mental equivalents — behind the overeating. And, as I've said, that isn't always easy.

A number of causes or mental equivalents have been discovered as possible reasons why people overeat. Food can be used as a substitute for love. Or as comfort when one feels distressed or anxious. It can be grasped at to quiet inner dissatisfactions. Compulsive filling of the stomach can be done for protection, the resulting fat serving as a buffer between oneself and others, between a sensitive ego and a hostile-appearing world (You can't hurt me with all this extra weight around me). Gorging oneself can also be a habit acquired in childhood, caused by a parental attitude of "eat everything on your plate or else."

There are, of course, still other causes and two different people may have utterly different reasons for their overeating. But if you can't resist chocolate cake and ice cream when you think you ought to, you might give yourself a treatment like the following:

There is one Mind, one Intelligence, one Love, one Balance, one Beauty. And I am that Mind, that Intelligence, that Love, that Balance and that Beauty individualized, right here and right now. And I deny that I have any need for food other than for the essential needs of my body. I direct the Infinite Intelligence within me to neutralize, negate and nullify any patterns of thought in my subconscious mind which cause me to hoard food in the form of overweight, as protection against hurt, distress and anxiety or as a safeguard against real or imaginary deprivations. I know that all the love in the universe is mine and I affirm that that love materializes as people in my world — men, women and children whom I love and who in turn love me. My body takes the food I eat and converts it into health and energy and whatever is not needed for these purposes is eliminated. Therefore my body is perfectly proportioned and has perfect symmetry.

I release this treatment into the Law, knowing that the Law accepts it, works on it and demonstrates it in my experience immediately. And so it is.

Concluding with a phrase such as "And so it is" adds emphasis in our mind, helping to convince us of the truth in our words. And we may need a little convincing. After all many of us have been in bondage to opposite beliefs most of our lives.

Will one treatment do it? Is one treatment sufficient to bring about the demonstration we desire — and "immediately," as we say at the end? Theoretically, yes. Theoretically we change form (conditions, relationships) the instant we say a treatment. And, of course, immediate demonstrations do happen. More frequently, however, we find a time lag between our treatment and its manifest form. Ernest Holmes believed the lag to be the time it takes the person saying the treatment (or for whom the treatment is said) to really accept the new idea, to really change his or her consciousness.

But as I said, treatments do manifest immediately and I can recall numbers of them that did, in the years of my teaching.

I remember especially one case of mine, that of a little old lady who came to me in the early days of my practice. Her story is one I cherish both because of the elements of humor in it and because it so perfectly illustrates this point about changed consciousness. I gave her one treatment and one treatment only. But she had such a simple conviction that it was going to work — she was so receptive to its immediate and complete demonstration — based, I must admit, on somewhat of a misunderstanding — that the change in her consciousness was also immediate and complete. And the corresponding change in her life was therefore just as immediate and complete. I see her now and then at a meeting or lecture and when I do I try not to say anything that could cause her to question.

She drifted into my office, the day of her appointment. At that time she was a colorless wren of a woman dressed in a snagged and baggy sweater and a nondescript skirt that hung unevenly. She wore no make-up. Her lips were blanched and dry. Her hair was a listless, faded brown.

Settling into the chair opposite me she folded her hands in her lap. The chair isn't big but she was so tiny and frail-looking that she managed to make it appear big.

I asked her name and she told me, "Norma Aarons."

Then she said, "I was at your noon lecture. A week ago. And you said, For Heaven's sake, if you've got a problem that's making you miserable, holding you back, keeping you from being happy, do something. See one of the people who teach here, if you can't do it yourself. Get it off your chest.

Tell whoever you see the whole story. Once and for all. Treat it out. Know that it's finished. Done with. Know you can start over. Free of the past."

Had I said that? In just that way? It sounded a lot like me and yet . . . .Well, yes, I finally acknowledged to myself, I do tend to wax overly enthusiastic sometimes and get carried away and this could have been one of those times. Zealot that I become on occasion I could have oversimplified in an effort to emphasize the necessity of clearing out the closets of the mind of the cluttered encumbrances of the past. An essential part of what I teach is the importance of being a today person in a today world.

But once? Could I possibly have implied that merely talking about a problem and giving one treatment for it would clear it up? Any problem? For anyone?

"Yes, you did," she suddenly insisted with a hint of belligerence that contrasted oddly with her meek deportment. "That's what you said. Exactly. Tell it, you said. Treat it out. Know you can start over. Free of the past."

She had sensed my uncertainty. I quickly followed my own teaching, straightened out my thinking and reminded myself firmly that whereas one treatment didn't always do it for everyone, it could definitely do it for her. If she believed strongly enough that getting her problem off her chest and one treatment was going to set her free — why, then it was. Nothing on earth could stop it from happening.

"I teach and lecture a good many hours each week so it's hard for me to remember everything I say," I explained apologetically. "But the essence of what you tell me I said is true."

She was satisfied. "I guess I'd better get started then," she murmured and sighed.

She sat there in that chair that was too big for her and she started. "When I was five years old both my parents were killed in a train accident."

She began with that tragic piece of information and she went on from there, carefully, methodically, meticulously going through her life history, year by year, recounting the failures she'd made, the troubles she'd encountered, the losses she'd sustained.

Once or twice I felt I ought to stop her and I tried but she didn't even hear me. Luckily I had no other appointments for the day. When her time was technically up she had only reached the events of her early forties.

She told about the aunt who had brought her up, who had hated her and resented caring for her and the additional financial burden her presence had placed on a family already at subsistence level. She told of being given away at ten to a childless couple her aunt knew, of being exploited by them as household help, of running away three years later, of being picked up by a man in a truck who'd taken her to his shack on the outskirts of a small town in Tennessee, of how he'd stayed with her just long enough to get her pregnant and delivered of a child before one day driving away in the truck and not returning, of how she'd supported herself and the baby until another man came along, of how she'd married this one, lived with him until four babies later when he too had disappeared, of how three of her children had died young and of how, of the two who were living, a son and a daughter, the daughter was a drug addict and the son an alcoholic.

They piled up. Tragedy on tragedy. In all they added up to one of the ghastliest lives imaginable. She spoke quietly, without self-pity, with a kind of numb detachment and, I was sure, without exaggeration.

When she'd finished she leaned back against the chair, breathed with great relief and said calmly, "Well, that's done. I can't think of anything more."

I was glad for that. I couldn't have taken much more. I felt punch drunk.

"It's a relief to know none of it's going to bother me from now on," she confided. "It sure used to. Kept me from doing all sort of things I wanted to do. Kept me so down I didn't have the heart."

I swallowed and said, "Fine. Great. All these things

you've told me about — from this moment you are free of them. Not by your just forgetting them but by you and me knowing together that all their power to hurt, to cause pain, is gone forever. From this moment yours is a consciousness of the now. You live in the now, you work in the now, you think in the now, you experience in the now. You are a contemporary person."

I said a good deal more but that's the gist of it. It was years ago and I don't recall the exact words. And, of course, I ended by giving her a treatment.

When she left my office she didn't drift out as she'd drifted in. She walked with purpose, her head high, her shoulders straight.

A few months later I was having coffee with a couple of friends who are also students and one of them, Griselda, asked, "Have you seen Norma Aarons lately?"

I had to be reminded of the woman who went with the name. When I did remember I shook my head. "I only saw her once."

Griselda laughed. "I know about the once. You'd never recognize her. If you did see her. She's had her hair dyed. Styled too. She has all new, today-styled clothes. She wears make-up. Looks years younger. Kind of almost pretty. And she's gone out and found herself another job. A lot better than the old one. More money. Better working conditions. And she's also doing volunteer work to help rehabilitate drug addicts. But the biggest change is she's happy. She sort of radiates."

"Wonderful."

"Yes, but you know what else? She's running around telling everyone that her whole life is different and what happened is — well, you go see this man, Eric Pace; you see him once and you tell him all the awful things in your life, get them off your chest. And he listens, talks to you, gives you a treatment and from that moment your whole life changes."

I pointed a finger at Griselda. "Listen, you," I told her

seriously, "don't you dare tell her otherwise. Don't you dare tell her anyone ever comes more than once. I must have said something about once at a noon meeting and she took me at my word. She believed the change was going to happen. She believed totally. Simply. She didn't have the slightest doubt. Her mind accepted that her life was going to change and it did. Her change of consciousness was complete so the change in her life was complete."

Griselda had sobered. "But how do you know she isn't going to find out sometime? By accident, if no other way?"

"I don't, of course. But if she ever does I'm sure that by that time the new way of thinking will be so normal to her that she won't care how it came about."

I don't know whether Mrs. Aarons ever has found out that there'd been a misunderstanding of sorts. Or was it a misunderstanding? Did she understand what at the moment she needed to understand? At any rate the last time I saw her she hadn't reverted to the drab, beaten little old lady who once sat in my office.

Total and immediate, Mrs. Aarons' kind of demonstration is what we all should aim for and, moreover, expect. But not achieving it should in no way discourage us or cause us to give up. I agree with Mr. Holmes' explanation about the delay between treatment and manifestation as being the time it takes us to accept the new idea (after all, it's logical that if we've been accepting an idea for ten, twenty or thirty years, it may take a bit of time to accept its opposite) but in my classes I enlarge on that explanation.

What we want to demonstrate very probably consists of a number of components, constituent parts, which must come together to make the whole. And I believe that the time lag is sometimes the length of time it takes the law of cause and effect, which knows every person, place and thing, to bring the parts together and fit them into a whole.

I'll have more to say about this law of cause and effect later.

For whatever reason, then, it is often necessary to repeat

a treatment and I tell my students to repeat any treatment they are giving themselves once, twice, a hundred times — as many as it takes — until what they're treating for shows up in their actual experience. If you are treating for a job, for example, the treatment cannot be said to have manifested itself (demonstrated) until you actually have a job.

But I would caution you in regard to this matter of repetition. Be careful not to let your treatments become mechanical and ritualistic. Rituals tend to take on an emotionless monotony. And, I remind you again, you are changing consciousness, your own consciousness. And emotion, especially strong emotion, is a vital factor in changing consciousness.

Therefore, if you do find it necessary to repeat a treatment for the same thing, such as health, always try to vary it a little. Each time you speak it aloud to yourself try to put as much desire for the health you want into your thought as you can muster.

Try, also, when you affirm that you have health, to feel as much conviction, faith, belief, that you do indeed have it as you can possibly manage. And try to feel it with progressive intensity in each successive treatment.

And if you're unable to summon any real belief and conviction, at least speak your treatment in a tone of belief and conviction. Doing so will help you gradually to acquire and strengthen such feelings within you and the more your belief and conviction grow, the more your consciousness changes.

If doubts and fears keep creeping in to discourage you, either during the treatment or later, treat them out as you would treat to get rid of any other negative. Just say to yourself in a firm voice, My own doubts and fears do not stop this treatment from demonstrating. Gone. They are gone. Out of my mind as of this moment.

Finally, if they persist in remaining, turn your attention to something else. Let the treatment be for awhile, knowing that it is just a matter of time. Doubts and fears cannot remain in a mind that is being retrained.

Treatment should be done daily for improvement in all

the general areas of our life, health, finances, relationships, work and all other experiences that make use of our talents and abilities. And preferably such general treatments should be scheduled at about the same time each day. An excellent and probably a convenient time for many people is after they awaken in the morning or before they go to sleep at night.

Such a general treatment could be along these lines:

I realize there is a great cosmic Principle, a Power, an Order which permeates the entire universe and is ever creating it, ever evolving it into higher and higher levels of perfection. And I know that I am part of that cosmic action of Life, my intelligence is some part of Its intelligence. It is thinking through me, as me; my mind is part of the Universal Mind which endows with Its intelligence all energies, all substances, all created things throughout the cosmos. And I also know that all wisdom, all power to solve any problems that may confront me, now and in the future, in any area of my life, are available to me and I realize that whatever I may need is immediately supplied to me as I accept it. And this I do, willingly, gladly. And so my good, the solution of any problem that may ever arise, is available to me and I accept it thankfully.

I relax and allow a new understanding to fill my mind. I let go of all hurts, negative beliefs, worries and insecurities. I let go of anything that could cause difficulty in my life, whether it be of health, of supply, of relationships with associates, friends and loved ones or of the expression of my talents and abilities.

And so my health is perfect, radiant health.

My supply is available and unlimited and ample for my needs.

My relationships with associates, friends and loved ones are firmly based, secure and loving.

My total use of all my talents and abilities achieves new, fulfilling levels of self-expression.

I commit this to the Creative Law of cause and effect, which does the work, and so it is.

When you first begin to use the technique of treatment you will very likely be interested primarily in changing one or more specific conditions that have been troubling you acutely, such as recurring headaches, a situation of tension between you and a loved one, or maybe a boss, the lack of money to buy a new coat or a car, a stomach ulcer or a state of painful and crippling arthritis.

Specific treatments are necessary, of course, especially in the beginning when you are apt to have a number of such problems with which to deal. And, naturally, whenever a specific problem does appear you should treat for it immediately. You should not put it off to some scheduled time. And if it's not convenient to say it aloud, then say it silently. Ideally you should give yourself a treatment any time you feel the need for one. Silent treatments can be given anywhere, anytime.

But you should think of Science of Mind not merely as a solver of problems of the moment. You should think of it as a way of life, a permanent part of your everyday existence. Only by so doing will you achieve the maximum good it has to offer.

And don't wait to use treatment until you feel you thoroughly understand how to do one. Don't put off trying to use the technique until, for example, you have finished reading this book. Begin right now. You will learn as you do. Your ability to form your thoughts into a treatment will grow with each effort you make. And as you begin to demonstrate, your belief too will grow. Each treatment makes the next treatment easier to formulate. Each demonstration increases your conviction that you can make another demonstration.

Now to get back to the creative law of cause and effect — since knowing that such a law exists is what enables us to control the circumstances of our lives through treatment— I think it's a good idea at this point to elaborate on what the Law is and how it functions. We cannot answer the why of it any more than we can answer the why of any other law of nature. It just is.

But as to what it is — well, it could be described as a mirror, a reflector of the inner onto the outer. And it is the producer of the forms, conditions, relationships and situations in our world. It functions according to our directives. We can direct it by making active, conscious, rational choices and get what we want from life. Or we can direct it by not directing it and take what comes as the result of our whims, impulses, irrational actions and choices, or the choices of others. Either way we are always directing it.

So we can be master. Or we can be victim. We have the option.

And, again, like any other law of nature, the law of creativity or the creative law of cause and effect does not have a choice of its own. It must function as it was designed to function. (Imagine the chaos of a world in which the law of gravity had a choice as to whether it would work as it was designed to work.) That is why we cannot plead or bargain with it. That is why we say it is inexorable and immutable. And that is why, if we want to be happy, healthy and successful, we must conform with the way it operates. Working as the scientist does, on the assumption that for every effect (such as disease) there is a knowable cause (an inner thought pattern of dis-ease) we are able through treatment to change effect by changing cause. In the case of ill health we are able to achieve health by changing the inner pattern of disease to one of ease.

By its very nature the Law must produce effect for cause.

But here we should understand that evil (illness, poverty, failure) is not created by Absolute Mind, Infinite Intelligence. How could it be? Is it logical to believe that an Infinite Intelligence which is in all, through all and as all, would create a force to work against Itself, to cause Itself suffering and pain? I think not. Evil is created by man's ignorance and misuse of this law of creativity. Evil is not an entity in itself. Evil is man's negation of the good.

Realizing this truth we should be our own worst enemy if we did not strive to use the Law as it was intended to be used — for our good. As we should be fools not to rejoice in its predictability, dependability and unchangeability.

Finally, no discussion of the law of creativity is complete without going into the principle of attraction, which is a sort of corollary to the Law itself.

The principle of attraction can be stated in a number of different ways but I think of it thus:

Each of us projects a thought atmosphere. This atmosphere is a reflection of what we think, both consciously and unconsciously. And it is this atmosphere which attracts to us what we experience in our outer world. If, for example, our thought atmosphere projects love, health, good fortune and happiness, we are going to attract love, health, good fortune and happiness in our experiences.

On the other hand, if our thought atmosphere projects anger, misery and bitterness, we are going to have experiences that fill us with more anger, misery and bitterness.

Most of us, I'm sure, are aware of this principle of attraction, though we may never have thought of it as a principle. We see it operating daily. As an illustration I'll use an imaginary but not so unusual case of two businessmen who are each seeking to obtain a loan in order to enlarge his business.

Both men go to the same local bank to apply for the loan. One businessman projects self-worth, confidence, belief in himself and in the future of his business. He is Success personified. Now, I'm not talking about the faker or the bluffer who puts on an act. I'm talking about the man with genuine self-esteem.

The other businessman projects doubt, fear and uncertainty. He is Failure personified.

Now, suppose you were the president of that local bank, which of the two men would you be more inclined to give the loan to? You may sympathize with the latter man but if you often give a loan on the basis of sympathy rather than on the basis of the likelihood of its being repaid and with interest, I'll venture to predict you're not going to be a bank president any great length of time.

As for me, if I were the bank president, I'd have to give a loan to the successful businessman and to refuse one to the man who projected doubt, fear and uncertainty.

I guess that's one reason why I'd never choose to be a bank president. Because I do sympathize with the unsuccessful businessman. I sympathize with anyone whose basic thought atmosphere projects doubt, fear and uncertainty. And not just because I know how unpleasant such emotions feel. But because I know how much more unpleasant are the experiences they inexorably lead to.

I sympathize but I also know that there's a technique he can learn and practice and that if he learns and practices that technique he can be just as successful as his fellow businessman.

I guess that's the real reason I'd never choose to be a bank president or anything other than what I am. I get too much satisfaction out of being a teacher of Science of Mind, a teacher of a technique that makes for ease, not dis-ease in the mind and in the body and in the world of affairs.

I shouldn't like refusing anyone a loan.

I like to see people happy. I like to see people healthy, productive and successful.

CHAPTER VII

Overcoming Obstacles
to Reaching Your Goals

Suppose you have been using the technique of Science of Mind over a period of time to change some condition in your life and no change in that condition has occurred. Let's say you have been "treating" (giving yourself a treatment) for prosperity and no change in your finances has taken place. Are you going to tell yourself that maybe the technique works for some people but that obviously it doesn't work for you and then give up, stop treating?

You can, of course, and you may never be any worse off financially than you are now but you are not likely ever to be any better off. The creative law of cause and effect exists and denying its existence is not going to change that fact. Your lack of prosperity is due to some thought pattern of want, scarcity, limitation or poverty in your consciousness and until you change that thought pattern you are not going to change your financial condition very much.

The Law is no respecter of persons as human laws sometimes seem to be. It works for all alike. It doesn't just work for a handful of lucky people or the good, the just and the chosen few. It works for everyone and all the time. It is indeed presently working for you, although in a negative way if you are in the negative experience of privation.

So rather than giving up, the wiser course of action is to examine what you are doing or failing to do that may be keeping your treatment from demonstrating. Some things that follow I have touched on before. They'll bear repeating.

A treatment can fail to demonstrate for a number of reasons. One of the most obvious reasons is that it becomes nullified by an opposite thought or emotion immediately after it's been said. For example, you give yourself a treatment for prosperity and immediately after you finish, you begin to worry because you don't have enough money to pay the rent or to make some needed repairs on your automobile.

You have affirmed in your treatment something to the effect that you have money in ample supply, that you have plenty to meet all your needs and desires, that money comes to you in large amounts and that you use it wisely and consistent with good. And, if you have followed my instructions, you have said your affirmations with as much conviction, faith and belief as you could command.

But hardly have you concluded before you fall back into the old ways of thinking. What are you going to do about the rent? How are you going to get the car fixed? You never have enough money. What are you going to do? Why can't you make money like other people? you ask yourself.

And if you're like most people the strength of emotion you put into fretting and lamenting far outweighs that which you put into the positive emotions you were able to summon up in your affirmations. Most of us put more emotion into worrying about a problem than we put into taking steps toward its solution.

Moreover, unless you realize what you're doing, check yourself and reverse the trend of your thoughts, you are probably going to spend a great deal more time in the worrying state than you spent on your treatment. It scarcely should come as any surprise to you, then, if your finances don't improve. You have not permanently changed the thinking that caused your lack of money in the first place.

It's easy to change one's mind for a moment but for the technique to work at maximum effectiveness one has to keep his or her mind on the affirmative idea that one has placed in the treatment. If there's any discipline in Science of Mind this is it — keeping one's mind on the affirmative idea. I cannot stress this point too strongly. Keeping one's mind changed is a vital factor in demonstrating the new condition, relationship, situation or whatever it is that one is treating for.

I know a man whom life seemed to have destined to become a store manager. But his love was music and in an agonizing moment, against the conditioning of a lifetime and against the wishes of his parents and all his relatives, he made a decision to become a voice teacher. Thereafter he never swerved from that decision, in spite of the years of difficulty, loneliness and hard work that followed.

Today he is one of the top men in his field and once, at dinner, he told me how he came to be doing the work he loves.

He grew up at a time when and in a section of the country where for a man to make music his career was practically unheard of. As a fairly young child he had pleaded so long and so passionately to be allowed to take voice and piano lessons that his parents had finally given in, although reluctantly and with the hope that he would soon outgrow his infatuation and turn his attention to more manly pursuits.

Instead, because his was a great and natural talent that couldn't be denied, he devoted himself increasingly to it, withdrawing more and more from the activities, games and hobbies in which other boys his age were engaged.

His father tried to interest him in what the older man considered masculine things, insisted on their going camping together (which the youngster hated), took him fishing (which he disliked but tolerated) and hunting (which he loathed and which frightened and sickened him). His three uncles also did their part to assist in diverting him from his strange "effeminate" preoccupation but were no more successful than his father.

Inevitably he became known as a sissy and slightly odd, "that queer boy of Essie's and Tom's." The situation was bad enough on the surface but what made it worse was that he was the only male child of his generation, not only in his immediate family but in the tightly-knit larger family unit that consisted of his father's brother and his family and his mother's two sisters and their families.

In addition each of the eight adults had an equal financial share in a large department store several hundred miles west of where he lived. At the time it was being managed by his paternal uncle but everyone had always expected that he would go into it on his graduation from high school, to be trained by his uncle to be his assistant, and for total command on his uncle's eventual retirement.

He didn't fight the plan at first. High school and graduation seemed very far away. But when he finished grammar school he realized that he had to do something. He couldn't go into the store. He had to continue with his music, use it in some way. How he didn't know. All he knew was that when he said "use" he didn't mean relegate it to an afterwork pleasure. It was his whole life and if there was no way by which he could make his living with it, why, then, he'd just have to starve.

He talked to his parents.

Tears, angry silences and bitter quarrels filled the next four years. At last, unable to reconcile them and worn down by their misery and disappointment in him, and by the pressure of his relatives, he agreed, as he expressed it, "to let them imprison me."

Two weeks after his high school graduation, with all arrangements made, a train ticket in his wallet, he packed his suitcase to head west.

That night his two maternal uncles and their families all visited to say goodbye. When they had gone he went up to his bedroom to sleep. He had left his packed suitcase on his bed and as he lifted it to remove it so that he could lie down, he suddenly thought, What's to stop me from taking it down to the station tomorrow and boarding a train that goes east instead of west? What's to stop me from going in the opposite direction? Maybe to New York?

In his mind he visualized the towering buildings he'd seen in photographs of New York City. So immense, that city. Surely he could find something to do with his music there.

Then he remembered the scene in the parlor downstairs, less than an hour ago, with his parents and relatives sitting around, discussing his trip and his future in the store. And he said to himself with a strange new clarity, I've been letting them do my thinking most of my life. I've been letting them make my choices. Decide my life. According to what they want. According to what's convenient and best for them. They'll find someone else to work in the store. They don't really need me. But I need me. I'm all I've got and if I have to give up my music I've destroyed the part of me that's really me. I'll be forever alienated from myself.

What have I got to lose? If there's no place for my music in New York, I'm no worse off. There wasn't any place for it where I was going either.

And that's what he did, the very next morning. He took his suitcase and boarded a train for New York City.

The first few years were really rough, he told me, and he had to work at all kinds of jobs to support himself and put himself through Juilliard School of Music but he never let himself look back, even in the most difficult moments or when he was sick with loneliness.

All of this must have occurred fifteen years or more ago. At the time, he realizes now, he was using the principles of Science of Mind, without knowing the teaching. Today he is an enthusiastic adept of it.

To get back — closely allied to the mistake of not keeping one's mind on the affirmative idea is another error which can also be responsible for a seeming failure in treatment. Remember that when you make a choice in your mind the creative law of cause and effect immediately goes to work to produce whatever it is you have chosen. Your new choice is a cause and the Law begins to create an outer effect like the inner cause. But if you are always changing your choices, always changing your directives to the Law, then every effect that it starts to produce will be aborted.

The result will be that you will get no one effect but a confusion of effects.

In my classes I illustrate the blunder in this procedure by telling the students to imagine that one of them represents the Law and that as the Law he must naturally function as it functions, which means that he must immediately do what I tell him to do since that's the way the Law works. Then I go on and say that he and I are going to pretend to prepare a room for a luncheon after class. The room has a number of chairs, two long tables, dishes, a refrigerator and a sink.

I am directing the operation, I tell them, and my first directive is, "Put tablecloths on the tables so we can lay the place settings."

The student starts toward a table but before he can reach it, I say, "First, push the chairs back against the wall, out of the way."

The student puts his hand out to push back a chair but I stop him with, "Wait! I forgot. We've got to phone the store for some tins of juice and put them in the refrigerator so they'll be cold when we want them."

The student walks toward the phone but I call out, "No, that's not so important as making sure all the dishes are clean. Better examine them and wash any that need washing."

The student turns toward the dishes but immediately I direct him back to putting on the table cloths.

And so it continues.

Is the student, I ask the class, ever going to get anything done? Is the room ever going to be prepared for our luncheon?

There is always much shaking of heads and an audible "no" or two.

Indeed, no. Unless I stop changing my directives to the student, nothing at all is ever going to be accomplished.

The same is true in treatment. Try not to keep changing your directives to the Law unless your new choice is a carefully selected preference and not a mere whim.

A third reason that a treatment may not become manifest is that the treatment is glib and by that I mean that the one who is giving it is saying it off the top of his head. The attitude behind it is one of "wouldn't it be nice if" rather than one of strong desire; such as when someone treats for a house in the country with a garden and a swimming pool because he has seen a picture of that sort of house and thought it looked pretty and that maybe he'd like to have a similar one some day.

Another example of a glib treatment is one that is given for something a person really can't conceive of himself as ever actually having; such as when someone is treating for a million dollars, although he has never at any time had more than a hundred dollars in his possession.

A fourth reason why a treatment may fail to demonstrate is that a person may not be willing to give up the thing that is holding the demonstration back. I have a young married couple who've been coming to me for help in establishing a better relationship between them but neither of them is willing to give up getting the better of an argument or refraining from attacking the other when an opportunity presents itself. They both want to keep the same old personality traits that are going to have to go if their relationship is ever to improve.

In this same area is the treatment that fails because the change a person consciously wants to make is one which subconsciously he is strongly resisting. A man may, for example, want to give up smoking because he knows it is endangering his health. He gives himself a treatment or two and nothing happens so he decides to try a little will power instead.

Unfortunately, as I've said, will power sets up a battle between the conscious and the subconscious which merely serves to keep the desire to smoke alive in one's emotions; so the man continues to smoke but now he begins to feel guilty and worse still, he begins to look on himself as weak, spineless, ineffectual.

What a concept of himself to put into his subconscious! Think of the outer experiences that can only result from such an inner thought pattern!

No, the thing to do when you find your conscious and subconscious at war is to be patient with yourself. Don't try to browbeat yourself into submission. Keep on treating and at the same time, calmly, easily, without straining, imagine yourself (if you too are trying to give up smoking) as a person who no longer needs the security and comfort of a cigarette, who no longer needs a cigarette to act as a friend and companion (which is what cigarettes do for some people).

The clearer image you can conjure up of yourself as a non-smoker, at the same time that you are treating to be free of the desire to smoke, the simpler will be your task of breaking the habit. Treatment, patience with yourself and calm persistence in picturing a successful outcome to your treatment will do more to bring the thought patterns in your subconscious in line with your conscious wish than any amount of will power.

Six other pitfalls to be wary of in treating are closely related to the six steps of treatment itself and I could name a number of instances where each was responsible for interfering with the successful objectification of one of my own treatments, until I caught my mistake and rectified it. The instances are few and far between nowadays because much of my thinking along these lines is permanently changed. But in the early days, when I was a beginner, I was like every other beginner, often plagued by an inability to throw off old ways of thinking, doing, feeling.

First, when, in step one of the technique, I defined the one great Power as Infinite Intelligence, Absolute Mind, God, First Cause or however I had chosen to call It at the time, I would find myself defining It in human terms. Oh, I don't mean specifically, in words, either vocal or silent, but in old mental concepts.

So I understand when my students tell me how difficult it is for them to get over thinking of this great Source of all good as a being, a sort of glorified person, a heavenly father, located in a place outside the earth plane, perhaps sitting on a golden throne, a male, a female, a male-female, possessed of human characteristics and human standards, capricious, irrational, inflexible, full of whims, a player of favorites, responding to the wants and needs of one and ignoring those of another, capable of dealing out prompt and unwarrantedly harsh punishment to one person while letting another, guilty of the same or a similar transgression, escape with no retribution at all.

Whereas the Universal Mind, the Infinite Intelligence, the First Cause, the God, the one great Power we are talking about in Science of Mind when we refer to the original and only Source of good, order, peace, harmony, joy, love, health, prosperity and perfect self-expression is that creative principle which is present in all space and in all time, on this earth plane as much as anywhere and at this moment in time as much as at any other. And it is present in all, through all, as all. And it is present as the totality of all possibilities.

If we start with the premise that what we are dealing with is an Infinite Intelligence that has every possibility within It, then how can we doubt that It is equal to anything? Knowing that nothing is impossible to It, how can we worry whether It can solve our problems, restore our health, fulfill our needs and grant our desires?

Remember, then, we are not defining a Power that is of human form, limited or circumscribed in any way. We are defining a Power that is all there is, all there has ever been and all there ever will be. Everything that ever was, is or will ever be is an idea in this divine Mind. And nothing is impossible to It. This is the new conception we must train our minds to accept.

And, as in the first step of the technique, we must remember always to think of the Universal Mind, not in human terms, but as infinite, total and complete, we must, in the second step, think of ourselves too, not in human terms, but as the Mind, the Power, the Intelligence individualized. Which means we must stop seeing ourselves as of a certain age, color, sex, weight, height, health, background and with such and such problems, accomplishments, relationships and financial means.

Now I am not trying to deny that these facts may be true about us in our physical experience.

What I am saying is that in treatment we must rise above them and see and know ourselves, not on the human level, not on the relative plane, but as what we are in potential and in truth — the Power individualized. That is the only sure way to move out of past limitation into perfection, achievement and good.

Third, when we declare in treatment that all good, everything we want and need is available to us in the here and now and we accept it, we must recognize that here too we are not referring to the relative plane. We must learn to distinguish between the consciousness that knows a thing cannot help but materialize because we have mentally accepted it in our experience and, on the other hand, the consciousness that expects the materialized form to be there in front of us the moment we open our eyes.

If, for example, you are treating for a blue Mercedes Benz and are trying to convince yourself that when you open your eyes it's going to be right there, in the room with you, what is your mind going to say? It's going to say, It's not possible. It can't happen. Right? And if you work this way you are working against yourself, against your mind's total acceptance that the car is going to appear in its logical time-space sequence.

'Here and now,' then, in the context of treatment, and on the level of the absolute, means that whatever it is you want is already available because the energy of Life is always present and always available to take form for our use. 'Here and now,' on the level of the relative means that — if you have been treating for a blue Mercedes Benz — you are aware that numbers of blue Mercedes Benzes exist, either in potential or actual form, one of which can become yours.

Or, if what you're treating for is a job, you realize that among all the people needing secretaries, all the agents needing clients, all the companies needing executives, all the stores needing help, all the offices needing specialized personnel, there is one that has a job you can fill.

All of treatment is done on the level of the absolute where the totality of all possibilities exists and where you are knowing (remember treatment is always done in the present) that among all these possibilities what you want and need is already yours in the thought patterns of your mind. And when it is already yours in the thought patterns of your mind, it has to become yours in form, though you must, of course, try to maintain "the knowing it is already yours" attitude when your treatment is over.

A fourth area to watch is that of denial. Don't harp on the denial. When denial is necessary because of the strength of the hold the negative experience has on you, make your denial quick and decisive. Get it over with. Don't linger on it. If you do, you are working non-therapeutically. You are emphasizing the negative.

Many of my students find another aspect of denial one of the most puzzling points to grasp. "How can I deny," they will ask me, "that I'm sick when I'm in so much pain and I feel so awful?" Or, "How can I deny I lack money when I practically don't have a cent to my name?" Or, "How can I deny that I'm lonely when I ache for someone to talk with, someone to care?" Or, "How can I deny that I'm bored and dissatisfied with my work when I feel that I don't belong in my job, that I'd prefer doing something else, that I should be accomplishing more but there's no opportunity?"

And so I have to go over it all again and remind them that the mistake they're making is that they're thinking on the relative rather than on the absolute plane. Their minds are concentrated on forms or relationships or conditions, instead of on the thought patterns that caused the forms, relationships or conditions. In treatment they should not be working with outer manifestations. They should be working with the inner thought patterns that caused the outer manifestations.

I am not denying, I tell them, that if you have a headache, you have a headache. What I am denying is that you have to continue to have that headache. I am denying the thought pattern that caused the headache. When that is gone the headache too is gone.

A fifth error can occur when we make our affirmations. I know people who mouth their affirmations, with no more emotion than if they were saying, "Brazil is a country where coffee is grown. Lots of people like coffee. I like it myself. It's good for breakfast, especially on a cold day."

As I've already tried to make clear, it is important to make your affirmations with emotion, with eagerness, with deep conviction, with desire. If you do not really desire something you are not liable to get it. It is thought plus feeling that change consciousness.

Oh, mouthing a treatment is better than nothing and doing so may eventually change your consciousness but the change isn't going to be very great or very soon.

At the opposite extreme are the people who concentrate their attention on how prettily they can express their treatment. They become actors and their affirmations are the lines of their performances. If you are searching for fine words you may not be intent on the meaning behind the words or the emotions you should be feeling through the words.

A final word on affirmations — in your treatments be specific about what you need and want but don't outline how you want it to come about. The moment you start outlining the way you want the thing to happen, you are limiting the sources from which your demonstration can come.

Not releasing the treatment, in step six, to the Law and trusting it to do the work, as beginners sometimes do, means that when the treatment is finished you continue to mull it over in your mind, wondering when and how it's going to come about, whether you ought to do this or that to help it along. You exhaust yourself trying to make it happen when what you should be doing is relaxing and letting it happen, knowing that the Law is doing the work and that you have only to take the action that is presented to you.

Mulling over treatments and not releasing them to the Law can be responsible for colds and congestion and when I find a beginner with such symptoms I frequently catch him by asking, "Have you been doing a lot of treating?" If the answer is, "Yes" — as it usually is; for beginners are so enthusiastic they often treat not only for themselves but for everyone they meet, from their best friends to the cop on the beat to the stray cat which ran down the alley with a dog chasing it — I suggest gently that if they were to release all the treatments they've been doing to the Law and stop trying to make them happen by their own human mind reasoning, the cold and congestion they're suffering from will very probably disappear.

One last thought on the matter — be aware of the possible pitfalls in treatment but don't dwell on them and don't worry about them unduly. It cannot be repeated too often that treatment is a flow of consciousness, a changing of patterns in the mind.

So give your treatments. Believe they are effective and if your demonstrations seem to be taking a little more time than you would wish, just keep saying to yourself, I have done the treatment. My demonstration is in the works. I will entertain no thought to the contrary.

And then, do just that. Entertain no thought to the contrary.

CHAPTER VIII

How I Achieved
the 'Impossible'

Now you are beginning to understand the principles and the technique of Science of Mind and you are applying them daily. Perhaps you have already had a demonstration or two — I can imagine your excitement.

But maybe you haven't and your disappointment is registering in the form of questioning, doubt, failing interest. It's a natural reaction but if you indulge it, then you really haven't understood a word I've been saying. The law of cause and effect is never suspended by anyone's doubt, questioning or lack of interest in it. If you truly want to demonstrate new and happier experiences in your life, you are going to have to persist until you change your mental patterns of causation.

Had I not persisted, despite years of seeming failure, I would still be a diabetic.

Earlier I promised you I'd tell you more about my personal story and I have, of course, gone into how in Science of Mind I found the answer to my long search for a way of life, a satisfactory philosophy, a guide and an aid for improving the quality of my experience, how my life began to change almost immediately and how after years of study in the many Science of Mind classes, under one of its greatest teachers, Dr. Raymond Charles Barker, I left the theatre so that I too could teach it and help others.

I have, however, saved what I think is the best part — the remission of my diabetes — until I felt that you were at a point in your knowledge where you'd be able to see how strikingly one of my own demonstrations illustrates what you have been learning.

Back in the hospital, when the doctors discovered how serious was my case of diabetes, they warned me that I would have to be on insulin the rest of my life and that what future I had would have to fit the limitations of my illness.

Well, as you know, I paid scant attention to their second dictum. But as to the first I had no choice. In order to stay alive I had to take insulin.

Again and again I have emphasized that for the most part one's mental attitude — one's thoughts and feelings — produces one's experience. And there's no question, as we've learned through psychosomatic medicine, that the body responds to one's mind and emotions. Experiments show that some people can consciously raise or lower their blood pressure. And doctors have long known that when an individual is suddenly confronted with what he considers to be a real threat to his person or his ego his adrenal glands will begin to pour adrenalin into his blood stream, to prepare his body for fight or flight. His eyes will probably tear so that they will not dry if he chooses to run. He may even have an instantaneous bowel evacuation, both to decrease weight and to permit all systems to concentrate on mobilizing their resources to meet the eventual choice — battle or escape.

And anyone who's a sufferer from hypertension and has gone to his physician for treatment has undoubtedly been cautioned to take it easy, to rest, get more recreation, stop worrying so much and avoid getting excited.

What is the physician really saying? He's saying that the patient's thoughts and emotions are influencing his or her physical body.

Most of us have experienced the stiff neck and tension headache that come from a hard day at the office. Or the butterflies in the stomach that appeared when we had to face an unpleasant situation. And many of us, I am sure, if we think about it, can remember having undergone a difficult period of some kind, one of loss or of strain, when our bodies began to respond to the stressful state of our minds by breaking down so that we fell ill.

If the loss wasn't too great and we were able to deal with it effectively or if the pressure and stress weren't too prolonged and we refused to let them take over our lives, the illness was probably mild, no more than a general malaise, or cold or a bout of flu.

But if the loss was one that touched us deeply and we were unable to handle it so that it did not absorb our thought and emotions, or if the tension and strain were protracted and we were unable to achieve relief from them, the illness was very likely much more serious, an ulcer, colitis, a heart attack, the onset of arthritis — or diabetes.

Now if you are a diabetic — as I was — you are almost certainly going to say to yourself — as I did — I don't believe a word of it. Anyway it can't possibly be true in my case. (Not excluding one's own situation, I've found, is probably the hardest thing for most people to do; I can't remember the number of times that someone has said to me, "Well, yes, I accept it's true in general but in my case . . ."). I never thought about getting diabetes, I assured myself. I never wanted to get diabetes. Who wants to have an illness that creates depression? Who wants to have an illness that makes you dizzy? Who wants to have an illness where you suddenly find that you're exhausted and you have to run for the chocolate bar you always keep near you?

Nobody, of course. It would have to be a very strange individual indeed who would want such an illness — that is, on a conscious level.

But on a subconscious level?

Well, I have come to accept the seemingly fantastic idea

that, not only is illness caused by patterns of thought and emotions, even the type of illness one acquires frequently is decided upon by a subconscious, if not conscious, choice.

I probably heard the words "mental equivalents" and "correspondences" at the very first Science of Mind lecture I attended. If I did they didn't mean anything to me. But in a few weeks I became very conscious of the expressions and as I began to understand that they stood for certain inner states that were the causes back of certain outer conditions and experiences, I eagerly set out to discover all there was to know about them.

I was still mostly thinking how knowing them could help me in my search for purpose, meaning, peace, and in my efforts to become more successful, as a person, a human being, and as a professional dancer, actor and director.

It hadn't yet occurred to me that I could and ought to be applying my new-found knowledge to improve my health as well as my affairs.

Of course I often heard other students excitedly discussing the possible mental equivalent back of this or that illness they or someone they knew had. As for me — well, I suppose you could say I had quite accepted the idea of being diabetic. Oh, I guess I minded but not all that much. That's the way it is, I'd tell myself. What's the use of complaining? It's just one of the breaks life hands out to some people.

The truth is that my illness was also providing me with a measure of attention. People were always saying, "You mean you can still dance and you're a diabetic?" As if that somehow made me great, as if I were some kind of hero, as if I had risen above a situation hardly anyone else could have managed to rise above.

And then one day in a Science of Mind class somebody asked the teacher, "What about diabetes? What's the cause, the mental equivalent, back of diabetes?"

Naturally I have never forgotten the answer:

"Lack of joy. A sense of not being happy deep inside. A feeling of loss. Treat for joy."

I have never forgotten the answer but my immediate reaction was to reject it, perfectly illustrating the "yes, but in my case" attitude.

Maybe, I thought. But not in my case. Wasn't everybody always commenting on what a sunny disposition I had, how easy I was to get along with, how pleasantly I treated others, how unruffled I was even in moments of crisis?

No, not me. It just didn't describe me. I was never depressed. At least, hardly ever. And when I was — well, diabetes causes depression. Any doctor will tell you that.

And as for loss—if I'd lost anything I hadn't the foggiest notion what it was and besides everybody loses something or somebody sometime.

Was I happy? Of course I was. I was in a very precarious occupation called theatre but my position in it didn't show any particular signs of being very precarious.

Mr. Sunbeam himself. That was me.

But after awhile I stopped rationalizing and decided, Okay, why not try it? What have you got to lose? And if it should work . . . !

So I searched through the Science of Mind textbook and found several prepared treatments on the theme of joy and I began reading them aloud daily.

A week passed and nothing happened except that I dropped a couple of the prepared treatments and ventured falteringly to make up a treatment of my own, specific for me, as I'd been instructed always to do eventually and as I've also instructed you to do.

Another week passed. And another. And another. Then months.

If there was any change in my physical condition none of the tests indicated the fact.

Many a time I got discouraged, as I've admitted. Sure I did. Many a time I thought of chucking the whole business. But then I'd admonish myself, What did you expect? Your type of diabetes is supposed to be incurable. The curable we do easily. The incurable probably takes a little longer.

I did change from a beginner, reciting my affirmations by rote: 'I am the joy of life. The joy of the Infinite Intelligence fills me. My consciousness is replete with joy. I have a deep inner happiness. There is joy in every cell of my body.' I became proficient at using the technique to create new and better and more self-convincing treatments.

And then one day my doctor took me off insulin and put me on Orinase, a drug that I could take by mouth. Two Orinase a day.

By then I considered my doctor a friend and I'd confided to him the technique I was using to try to bring about a cure.

He was probably skeptical to say the least but he had been encouraging me. Until I suggested that maybe I was beginning to make a demonstration.

"No," he said flatly. "You're probably taking better care of yourself. Sticking more to your diet. Being more sensible about the amount of work you take on. Don't get the wrong idea. Your condition is just as serious as it ever was. So don't you dare go fooling around. Doing something dangerous like trying to cut down on your medicine."

He was so concerned that I quickly assured him that I wouldn't. Besides I had too often heard my teacher deliver similar counsel on discretion to be unaware of when it was called for. Not too long ago he had said to a young woman during a class session, "While we believe that even serious illnesses such as the one you say you have can be cured by correct consciousness, we all have to work at the stage of mental and emotional development where we are. If you have not yet reached the level of consciousness where you do not need medicine — and apparently you haven't since your doctor says you still need it — keep treating for perfect health. But meanwhile take your medicine!"

More time passed. Months. A year. Two years. Three. All sorts of wonderful things were taking place in my life. The theatre continued to be extraordinarily kind to me. Success followed success. I danced. I acted. I directed. I was often so busy that I had to do the homework for my Science of Mind courses late at night or in the early hours of the morning before going to bed. I was now in the third year of study and more and more it absorbed my thoughts. Many of my old friends had followed along and were studying with me and I had acquired scores of new ones.

My health? I still had diabetes. I was still on two Orinase a day. Though sometimes I had the feeling that I was a lot better, even if the evidence of the tests for the amount of sugar in my system didn't bear me out.

Was I still treating after three years of seeming failure? Every day. Often I suppose out of sheer habit as much as anything else. Nevertheless there were days and weeks and even months when fresh conviction of eventual victory would keep me at it.

And then, gradually, I became aware that something very strange was happening to me. Day after day I was treating for joy and suddenly for the first time in my life I began to experience periods of depression, deep depression, and not momentary either. Depression that was like a flock of big, black clouds settling down around me.

A suspicion slowly crept into my consciouness that if I were a sunbeam I was only a surface sunbeam. Underneath, deep inside, I was unhappy, desperately unhappy. Underneath I felt an enormous sorrow, about what I had no idea. Underneath I had a sense of being badly hurt, in what way I was unable to discover.

I can write about it now but seven or eight years ago when these events were occurring I would never have exposed such feelings to anyone. I had created a mask for myself in my own mind, for the benefit of myself and others, and I could not have dropped my guard to reveal the real self behind the mask.

Sorrow. Hurt. Unhappiness. One or the other emotion would crop up over the most unlikely person or for the most unlikely reason. So I soon realized that whatever called them forth was merely a substitute for the true cause.

For instance, I went through an interval when I felt very

sad about my mother. Poor mom, I'd think, how terrible it must have been for her to be an immigrant, in a strange land, far from her own country, her own village. Having to learn a different language. And Italy's so much more conscious of family ties. What adjustments she's had to make! And then, working so hard all her life—having to bring up five children in the bargain—why, she's just never had a break.

The amusing thing, which I managed somehow utterly to overlook at the time, is that my mother has always been a bright, energetic, perfectly happy woman.

After I got over sorrowing over her I took on one of my brothers. After my brother, one or another relative became the target. After the relatives, my friends came in for their share.

It wasn't until I found myself almost in tears over four total strangers that I acknowledged that I'd kept all these things to myself too long, that I'd better talk to somebody, share them, see if that might help.

I was on a 10th Avenue bus at the time and along the route we had picked up a mother and her three dirty little children. The mother could have been any age but she must have been young because the three boys weren't even in their teens. She was fat, pushy, slatternly and given to swatting the boys indiscriminately whenever the impulse seized her.

The kids were boisterous, quarrelsome and undisciplined and their English was so bad they might never have seen the inside of a school, though I knew they must have.

Poor kids, I thought as I watched them, they haven't got a ghost of a chance. Such beautiful little faces and they're going to grow up tough and mean and illiterate.

A film began to cloud my eyes and that's when I sat up straight and said to myself, Man, this has got to stop. You have got to get to the bottom of this nonsensical behavior. How do you know those kids are unhappy and how do you know they're going to grow up tough and mean and illiterate? You'd better talk to somebody. Maybe Joan would understand.

When I reached home later that day I phoned my friend Joan and told her about the incident. Then I told her about a couple more.

"I sensed something of the sort was going on with you," she informed me when I'd finished, "and you've got to get over this sensitivity. You're tearing yourself apart."

"Thanks," I answered dryly. "Well, sure. I've been telling myself the same thing. Only I don't know what's behind it."

Joan was also in the third year Science of Mind course. "You know that doesn't matter. Treat it away."

"But I am. In a sense. Every day I treat for joy."

"Maybe that's it."

"Maybe what's it?"

"Maybe all the emotions are coming out that kept you from really experiencing joy and maybe you've got to deal with them and get rid of them before you're ever going to be able to feel joyful."

She was a very wise young lady but I couldn't admit it. "Great," I said. "I figured that out too. What I haven't been able to figure out is how I'm going to do it."

Joan ignored the tone of my voice. "You'll just have to keep treating. I'll do a treatment for you too. You'll have to keep working at it."

And work at it I did. I added a night treatment. And then I added a treatment before lunch. And, of course, whenever I began to feel the slightest bit depressed I'd give another.

I may have been carrying it to the point of absurdity in those weeks but I did seem to be managing to get control of my runaway emotions.

And then I made a startling discovery.

With no change of medicine, with no change of diet, with no change in the routine of my days, the sugar content in my blood was going up and down like a yo-yo, according to my mood! When I wasn't disturbed it was relatively low. When I was upset, depressed, sad or unhappy it skyrocketed.

My emotions were affecting my body. That emotions did

affect the body I had been hearing over and over again in my three-year study of Science of Mind and over and over again I had been telling others the same thing. I believed completely and yet I was stunned at the proof.

Another year passed, a year of great change in my circumstances.

I don't know when I first began to toy with the idea of leaving the theatre and becoming a teacher of Science of Mind, probably early in my second year of study, and as time went on the thought became an obsession.

But there were very real obstacles. I was a New Yorker and there didn't seem to be room for another Science of Mind teacher in the New York area. Moreover, even as a beginner I had to be able to depend on a certain amount of money to meet my obligations. I was a success in the theatre but could I duplicate that success as a teacher?

And then, unexpectedly each obstacle faded away and I found myself lecturing and teaching in the new headquarters in New York City.

That same year the doctor decided to try varying the dose of Orinase, and I made out, at least I did most of the time. For brief periods I'd have to go back to the regular schedule.

After five years of treating for health and joy I was travelling by subway one day to visit my sister when the blackest depression I had ever experienced hit me. I was bewildered. I hadn't had one in some time and I'd thought I had pretty much gotten them out of my system and now this king-size one appeared and settled down around me.

I had been studying "Three Magic Words," a book I was teaching at the time and my first thought was that something in the book must have disturbed me. So I went back over the pages I'd just read. But no, I finally decided, nothing I found there could be what was making me so sad.

Put the book away, something inside said to me, because it has nothing to do with the book. You have three quarters of an hour or more. Pretend you're sleeping and just see what comes to your mind.

I'd begun not to be afraid when something unpleasant from my subconscious seemed bent on revealing itself to me. I'd learned that when it was ready to come out that meant I was ready to handle it.

Closing my eyes I slumped down in my seat, tried to relax and clear my mind of extraneous thoughts. Screeching and rattling the subway train plunged and jerked and swayed ahead and my body followed along with it so that for awhile I couldn't free myself from the vague annoyance of the sounds and the movements.

But then everything receded and I was suddenly thinking of the three women, or perhaps I should say girls, with whom, to one degree or another, I had once thought myself in love.

People who know me well are always amazed at what they call my astonishing memory. I can remember such details as the color of a necktie worn by an actor in a show I cast fifteen years ago. Or that such and such actress was the one I saw in a certain play and who ran from left to right down stage and uttered the non-momentous line of, "Buzzy, he's figured it out."

An astonishing memory but as I bumped along in that subway car I couldn't even put into perspective the only three important romantic episodes in my life. I couldn't remember the time sequence in which the women appeared, their faces, their personalities—and the one I was to marry—except that she decided to marry someone else—I couldn't even remember her name!

When you are the possessor of an unusually keen memory and you can't remember the name of the girl you were to marry, there's something more than a little wrong.

And then as I recited to myself a series of names, trying to come up with the right one, I became aware of a painful feeling of hurt, of loss.

Moreover I knew that for once I was not substituting one situation for another. Emotions and the situations that had caused the emotions had come together with dramatic force.

Had I cared so much? I marveled. Why, I had even gone

to the girl's wedding and I had danced and laughed and joked. And when Gita, a friend of mine, had said, "Hey, shouldn't you feel sad or at least pretend to feel sad? After all, she's the bride but you're not the groom," I'd answered, "Sad? What about? She looks happy. I'm glad for her. Nobody can help these things. It happened. She found somebody else she likes better. That's the way it is."

Big, brave, generous, altruistic me—I must have been devastated and if I'd had any sense I'd have admitted it, at least to myself, stayed home from her wedding and let my feelings out. Howled, if that's what I felt like doing.

Loss. Hurt. Sadness. Great unhappiness. The pattern for diabetes had probably been laid down deep in my subconscious at that time and it was still there and I was going to have the diabetes until I got rid of it.

But wait, I was getting rid of it, wasn't I? Wasn't that just what was happening when all these things came up? Weren't they coming up, revealing themselves to me so that I could face them, deal with them and banish them never to bother me again? Of course.

No, there was still something else, something deeper, augmenting the first pain and grief and sadness I'd felt. Nobody had understood. That was it. Nobody had seemed to care or realize how hurt I was. Nobody had put an arm around me even for a moment and said, "Too bad, guy, I know how you feel. Losing your girl hurts like hell."

I pondered the need I'd had for comfort and sympathy and I felt angry and bitter. But then I had to concede, Who would have dared to commiserate with you? Who would have known you needed commiseration even if he'd dared? You and your false independence. People need each other, more sometimes than other times, but when have you ever let anybody know you needed them very much?

If you want to be given to, you have to accept, I reflected with a mixture of sorrow and relief.

Later when I reached my sister's house she made us both a cup of coffee and we sat down to talk.

"Mel," I asked, "what was the name of the girl I was going to marry?"

She stared at me, raising her eyebrows. "Are you kidding?"

"No, for some reason, I can't remember."

"Audrey," Mel said.

Of course. Audrey.

"Did you know how hurt I was when she decided to marry someone else?"

"Hurt? No. You didn't act hurt. I didn't think you cared really. Besides if any of us had worried about you, we knew you'd be okay. You were always the one to bounce back and land on your feet."

"I've got sad news," I said. "Sad for me, not you. I've just learned how vulnerable I am. I was plenty hurt and obviously couldn't feel or express it. And you know something else? I sorrowed over that girl, bless her, wherever she is, for two years, not that I was aware of it. Now I know that's what the numbness was. I guess I really never got over her until today. Or rather, not her, the hurt of rejection."

Mel put her hand over mine. "I'm sorry. But, you know, at nineteen . . . ."

"Nineteen or ninety," I said wryly and then suddenly a laugh welled up in me and burst from my lips. It wasn't a laugh of joy but it was restorative, healing.

Mel laced her fingers through mine and laughed too. Our hands clung together a moment. I think she felt very close to me and I know I felt very close to her.

Two weeks later my doctor said to me, "I can't quite explain it but something's happened. Your blood sugar level is definitely lower. I think we might try an experiment. I'm going to try putting you on one Orinase a day and see if you manage. Now, mind you, it's an experiment. You must keep strictly to your diet and work on your thoughts and emotions. And keep testing for sugar every day and if you feel the least bit bad, start taking the usual dose and phone me at once. Remember you've a strong hereditary predisposition to diabetes and that's a fact we always have to keep in mind."

The years of treatment and my persistence were finally beginning to pay off it seemed. I should have been elated and of course I was pleased but — well, perhaps the trouble was I didn't dare believe. I remember thinking as I left his office, Now what do I do?

The problem of diabetes had been with me a long time and all the ritual that went with it had become part of my daily existence. It was a bother and I had expected to be delighted to be free of it but what I felt instead was a sort of void I didn't quite know how to fill.

I needn't have concerned myself with that detail. Within a couple of weeks I knew the illness was back in my body.

By now the doctor was hopeful and enthusiastic. He was determined to have that cure. Whenever I showed signs of improvement he'd cut the dose from two Orinase a day. Whenever I had a relapse he'd put me back on my regular dose. During one appointment he said to me, "Have you ever examined yourself to see whether some of the old patterns of thought are still hanging around? Anything that would explain these ups and downs?"

"In a way," I admitted. "I don't think there's anything from the past but when I'm very tired or grouchy or crabby or if somebody hurts me or I feel unhappy, the test paper turns blue again (meaning an increase in sugar). My system responds poorly to certain types of emotions."

"Then why don't you see if you can avoid situations that cause them?"

"How? I live in an urban society. If I lived on a farm and only saw a couple of people a month . . . . And then there's my work. You know how many people my work brings me into contact with each week and how emotionally taxing it can be."

Even as I was speaking I knew the answer. I couldn't run away from people or my work. I didn't even want to. So the obvious solution — why had it escaped me so long? It wouldn't have escaped me very long in someone else — was to train myself to acknowledge and face these negative emotions the minute they appeared. Face them and say to them, I'll deal with you mentally but you are not going to affect my body. I'll admit that I'm hurt or afraid or sad or annoyed. I'll not pretend something doesn't matter when it does. I'll not deny I feel rejected when I do.

I think that was the turning point although many more months passed before the doctor could lower the dose permanently to one Orinase a day and I could remain free of symptoms.

At last I had a remission of my diabetic condition. Of course I know I'll always have to continue watching my emotions. I'll always have to try to stick to my diet but that's only intelligent; I ought to be even more rigid about it than I am.

Now and then, for periods, I go without even the one Orinase. When my mental and physical dieting are at their optimum, in spite of my hereditary predisposition, I am able to dispense with the Orinase completely, even as I work for the state of perfect health I know is my birthright.

It took ten years. Ten years, you may be thinking, is a long time to have to treat before one gets a demonstration.

But is it so long when the demonstration is the remission of an illness like diabetes?

CHAPTER IX

Some Basic Causes

Behind Health Problems

I believe that health is the birthright of everybody. I believe that the Infinite Intelligence, the Absolute Mind, the First Cause, created a perfect body prototype for each of us when It created us. I believe that if we keep our minds firmly fixed on the idea that within us is the reality of perfect health — whatever the outward appearances to the contrary — we can eventually manifest that perfect health, the one restriction being the level of our own human mind consciousness or that of the present human-race mind consciousness.

And I add the last, qualifying phrase only for the comparatively rare cases in which there have been disturbances in the genetic code, such as birth defects, the why of which science has not yet discovered, or where environmentally caused accidents or diseases have resulted in seemingly permanent body damage, such as the loss of a limb. I say 'seemingly' because many scientists are of the opinion that a man who has lost a leg should be capable physiologically of growing a new one, the way a tadpole does.

Yes, health has always been ours, is ours now and will always be ours. That is reality. It is reality because there is only one Power and that Power is perfect so Its entire creation must be perfect. It is reality because the Infinite Intelligence, knowing only perfection, can create only that which is perfect.

But Man, to whom the Infinite has given free will, can take that which was made perfect and by his own thoughts, feelings and actions make it seemingly imperfect. Yet, in spite of visible conditions of ill health, in the depths of our being there is a part of us — the prototype of perfection — that always remains untouched by what we or others have done or are doing to our bodies — or to our relationships or to our affairs.

I have obviously not, from the history of my own struggle against illness, always believed this. But I believe it now for I have seen the fact demonstrated, not only in my own life but in the lives of many of my acquaintances, friends and students.

Health is the permanent reality. Sickness or disease is a temporary experience. But most people cannot project their thoughts beyond their present, temporary experience. They are sick today so they fear they are always going to be sick. Most people are blocked from seeing what they want to see in the world of form (health) by what they actually do see (illness). Their minds can only dwell on the illness, on the pain, on the symptoms, on the handicaps that are a part of it.

And so, since, as Science of Mind teaches, it is thought and emotions which create form, by their thinking and by their emotions, they perpetuate their ill health.

We set our own limitations, whether they be those of bad relationships, frustrations in our work, lack of supply in our finances or dis-ease in our bodies.

Often when one of my students hears me make such a statement for the first time his or her hand will go up and a voice will despairingly protest, "But I just can't believe . . . . I never thought about having hypoglycemia (or asthma or eczema or whatever) until I got it. I think about it now, of course. How can I help it, now I've got it? But how did it come about in the first place? I know I didn't think about getting it. I just didn't."

And I smile, recognizing myself, recognizing all the others I've known over the years who have said, "Yes, but not in my case."

Then I explain again as so often I've explained before, "We're not saying there's an exact, precise, direct, one to one relationship between cause and effect, although such a thing does happen. It may be true that you have never thought of getting the hypoglycemia you tell me you have. Not as such. And certainly not consciously. But your thoughts must have been of illness of some kind. Accepted from something you read, saw or heard, maybe from a suggestion made to you by a parent, a doctor or a friend who casually remarked that you weren't looking well that day.

"Or you thought illness by wanting to escape something, gain sympathy and attention or by just plain wanting to take a rest from it all. Which is not to place blame on you or another. Placing blame gets us nowhere and only serves to increase the amount of time we spend going over and over our resentments and their sources, which in turn can only make us more ill.

"Or you occupied yourself with the kinds of thoughts that cause emotions that disturb the smooth functioning of bodily processes — anger, jealousy, hostility, depression, envy, self-pity. These feelings eventually produce illness of some sort.

"The point to remember is that all mind activity inevitably tends to create its physical correspondent. So an unhealthful and morbid mental state projects itself into the physical body, though not, as I've just explained, on a one to one basis. Actually, of course, it projects itself into our entire experience but at the moment we're talking about health and the physical body."

And then I usually try to give help for the protestor's personal problem. "I can't give you the cause in your particular case," I'll tell him or her. "Because I don't know anything about you — that is, I don't know you personally — and the precise cause back of the effect of any illness is individual to a large extent. By that I mean there is no universal cause for any specific illness. Just as psychiatrists have found that there are no symbols for the most part that are universally applicable to everyone's dreams. A symbol may mean one thing to you and another to me, depending on what we have come to associate it with through our individual experiences.

"However," I continue, "we in Science of Mind believe that, generally speaking, blood diseases like hypoglycemia and the diabetes I once had are caused by a lack of joy, not surface joy but deep, inner joy. I suggest that you treat for joy. I still do."

And it is usually when such an incident as this comes up that I take time to caution the whole class, as I would caution you too at this time. In the matter of analyzing what you think is wrong with your friends, what you think is the cause or mental equivalent back of any result, physical or otherwise that they have — please don't go around telling them why you think they're in the state they are, whatever it is.

Don't tell a friend, for instance, who has a bladder infection, that he's full of hostility he's holding back just like he's holding back his urine. Not because your analysis might not be correct, since, as psychosomatic medicine has discovered, repressed hostility often can be the cause back of bladder infections.

Don't do it because, first of all, your analysis may also not be correct in his or her case; and second, because it is really not your business to analyze what's behind the predicaments of your friends, unless you're trained for it and asked for help; and third, because you just might find yourself ending up with a black eye because some friend didn't appreciate the opinion you volunteered.

And now having done my duty and cautioned all concerned about not meddling in the affairs of friends as to causes and mental equivalents, I hasten to add that that same need for caution doesn't apply to one's own problems. If one has a bladder infection and treats himself against repressed hostility but it's not in his consciousness, he may not achieve a cure of the infection but he can do himself no harm.

So if you think you know a mental equivalent, try it. If it's correct, it can be very useful.

Though having it isn't vital; I'm sure I could have relieved my diabetes without knowing the mental equivalent for that condition, by just giving myself treatments for total health. Nevertheless I'm inclined to think the remission would have taken longer to accomplish.

On the other hand, a number of teachers in Science of Mind differ with me on this last point. And, although once psychiatry used to feel it couldn't cure without knowing the cause back of the illness, there are branches in that field today which simply work on changing the present harmful patterns in the patient's behavior that are responsible for his pain and trouble. They no longer dig into past experiences.

Still, I myself prefer to try to seek out causes or mental equivalents and I encourage you to do so also. Puzzling them out isn't usually all that hard, as I'll illustrate through a number of histories of cases I've had.

I well remember the woman in my first illustration, not only because she was beautiful but also because of her gracious manner. Her name was Olive Marston.

After the usual amenities during which I had to force myself not to stare at the exotic, china-doll face, framed in an incredible blue-black cloud of hair, I asked what her problem was.

She told me in a soft, pleasant voice, "I run a constant fever. Not dangerously high but high enough to be annoying and definitely debilitating. I've been to a number of doctors, naturally, but no one can find anything physically wrong. I've a friend in Science of Mind and she keeps lending me books about it. Then a few weeks ago — after much hinting — she came right out and urged me to come to see you. So" — she spread her long, slender, white hands in a graceful gesture — "here I am."

She didn't add, "Now, let's see what you can do," but

she might have for she leaned back with an air that was a combination of waiting and gentle skepticism.

I put several pertinent questions to her to find out how much she knew about Science of Mind and how much I might have to explain to her. Evidently, from her answers, she had carefully read the books her friend had lent her.

Under further questioning she also told me briefly about herself. I caught one remark I thought revealing.

When she had finished I asked if she really believed that thought produces form, that the effects in her physical world (her fever, for one) were caused by the patterns in her mind, that thought is cause and form is effect.

She hesitated. "Well," she finally answered, "it's an interesting concept and I'm inclined to think there's something to it but . . . "

'But, in my case . . . ,' I mentally finished for her.

And then, surprisingly, she announced firmly, "No, if it's true at all, it's also got to be true in my case."

Intelligent, objective and courageous, as well as beautiful, I thought. What a lucky man her husband must be.

"You're further along than most beginners," I commended her. "It's hard for most beginners to stop looking for outside causes. Most of them want to continue to justify whatever their problem is by blaming external factors. Learning to stop blaming people, places and things for our situation or condition and to look instead into the hidden recesses of our minds, into our own thought patterns — that's one of the toughest tasks for any of us to face.

"My father, my mother, my husband, my wife, my background — we trot out all the old excuses and then we're off to the races. Or 'If you'd been brought up in a ghetto like I was....' 'If you'd been brought up by two rich famous parents who were never around, like I was....' You'd be surprised, Mrs. Marston, how often the two extremes are used to justify very similar attitudes.

"But none of these are the causes of what's happening in

our lives. The causes are our reactions to the people or situations. The causes are the thoughts we're harboring about these people or situations, the emotions toward them we're clinging to."

"Look," — she leaned forward and her thickly-lashed dark eyes were very serious — "I've tried but I can't, can you? Can you imagine anything I could have thought or be thinking that could cause me to run this constant fever? I don't even know the illnesses that are accompanied by constant fevers. Except malaria and tuberculosis and there's no reason I'd ever have thought of getting either of them. Anyway, the fact is I don't have either of them. That's been established."

"You're making a mistake people frequently make, Mrs. Marston; Science of Mind isn't teaching that one must have thought about a specific disease in order to have gotten that disease. Though perhaps some of us teachers and some of the books fail to make that point as clear as it should be made. But have you ever read Frederick Bailes's 'Hidden Power for Human Problems'?"

She shook her head.

"He makes what I'm talking about quite plain. In fact" — I grinned — "I've often wished I could have thought of his explanation first. I take consolation that he was ahead of me in time. Anyway, Bailes says, and I'll have to paraphrase because I don't recall his exact words, that indeed people often have never thought about the particular illness they've acquired but that they have probably been dwelling upon thoughts that create within them the emotions of anger or hate or unhappiness or fear and that the 'parent' thought produces its own 'offspring.' We see the 'children,' which is to say, the illness, the poverty, the bad relationships or lack of creativity. In other words, we see the unhappy experiences in our lives. But rarely do we recognize the 'parent' without searching. That's the part I'd like to have said, that about the parent thought creating an offspring like unto itself but also different as human children are often similar but still different from their human parents.

101

"I like it because it's the true, wider meaning behind our belief that what happens in the inner world of thought is what determines what happens in our outer world of experience, form, affairs."

She leaned closer and asked softly, "And can you tell me what are the parent thoughts in me that create my offspring of fever?"

"I can hazard an educated guess, based on experience. From something you said when you were telling me about yourself. You'll have to decide whether my guess has any validity."

"How? How do I decide whether it has validity?"

"I think you'll sense if it's true."

"And if I don't?"

"I can always be wrong. There are no universal causes that apply to everybody. We are all individuals. We are all different. But work on the idea for awhile anyway. If it isn't the real cause it may reveal to you what is."

She nodded slowly. "I'll buy that. For the moment. Hazard your guess."

I hesitated. She was so beautiful, so well-mannered, so soft-spoken, the epitome of what is called a lady. But she was also sick and needed help. "I think," I said, "that the parent thoughts of your fever are intense feelings of anger, resentment, perhaps even hate."

She drew back. She looked horrified, incredulous.

"Against your mother-in-law," I went on. "Perhaps a little against your husband also. Because he doesn't protect you from his mother. But mostly against your mother-in-law because she dominates you."

"Oh, but it's not possible!" she whispered, her voice shaking. "I couldn't — I couldn't feel such things. Anger. Resentment. Hate. Oh, I'd be so ashamed if I thought . . . . Why, she's my husband's mother. My mother-in-law. How could I hate her? Maybe I get upset sometimes over things she says or does. But resent her? Hate her? Oh, no. No. No. That would be — terrible! Wrong! Sinful!"

"I'm sure that consciously you don't feel any of these emotions toward her," I said. "And I must disagree with you. Feeling such emotions is not something to be ashamed of. You're caught up in the old ways of thinking. The ways in which I gather you were brought up.

"In Science of Mind we don't think in terms of shame or sin. Anger, hate, resentment — to us having such emotions is not a sin. Ernest Holmes who as you know founded Science of Mind said, 'There is no sin but a mistake. No punishment but an inevitable consequence.'

"I agree with him, Mrs. Marston. Utterly. Thinking hate, resentment, anger is not a sin. It is a mistake. It hurts no one but you. But it does hurt you. It has hurt you. The inevitable consequence in your life — which is not punishment from an outside source but the inevitable consequence of your thinking — is the fever in your body."

She sat with her eyes cast down, her fingers tightly laced in her lap.

"Do you know, Mrs. Marston," I continued, "I can still remember when I first heard those words of Mr. Holmes. He lifted a tremendous burden from my shoulders. The burden of guilt we all feel when we're thinking in terms of sin. Because we've all hated, resented, been angry at some time in our lives. And if we continue to think in terms of sin — well, sins are formidable to overcome. Mistakes are not. Sins cause guilt. Mistakes don't. And guilt destroys what's left of our feeling of self-worth right when we need it most. Because a feeling of self-worth is necessary in overcoming anything.

"But when we think of such things as simple mistakes which have unpleasant consequences we don't wish to experience, then we begin to think in terms of the solutions, since we don't want the consequences. And that means we've more than half won the battle. I'd like you to think in terms of mistakes, Mrs. Marston."

Conflicting emotions kept crossing her beautiful face. Finally she asked, "What was it I said that led you to your guess?"

"You mentioned something your mother-in-law had said to you and you added, with an amused smile and half as though you didn't really mean it, 'I suppose I get a bit burned up when she says such things to me.'"

"Burned up," she repeated, raising her head. And then her dark eyes slowly widened and she murmured, "Why, of course. Burning up with anger. Burning up with hate. Burning up with resentment. How often people use such expressions."

"'He gives me a pain in the neck.' 'She makes me sick to my stomach,'" I contributed. "'I'm tired of carrying that burden on my back.' 'I feel as if I had the weight of the world on my chest.' Yes, the old sayings often do seem to contain more than a grain of truth in them. Though not always. And, of course, the real truth, in any event, is that it is not another person, another he or she, the world or the burdens that cause our trouble but our response, our reactions to them."

"What do I do now?" she asked, uncertainly. "If you're right, and I'm willing to concede you could be, what do I do now? I don't want to feel anger or hate or resentment. And I don't want to be sick. But my mother-in-law is a dominating person. Very dominating. And I'm not. It's hard sometimes . . . ."

"What do we do now? Work on the problem. I'll give a treatment and you begin giving yourself your own treatments against anger, hate, resentment. And you affirm that you are not dominated by anyone. You affirm that the Infinite Intelligence created you as a unique individual and therefore a person of unique worth.

"As for your mother-in-law — you don't have to let her dominate you, you know. As a unique person you ought to have a right to insist on being yourself. If you gently insist on that right, in time, I predict, your mother-in-law will recognize it."

"I doubt it." She faltered. "I doubt it. You don't know my mother-in-law."

"No," I admitted. "And maybe I'm wrong. Maybe she

won't. But I do know you can change your reaction to her. Which is the important thing. If you are determined to change it. And if you want to be well and free of fever."

"If," she repeated. "How can you say 'if'?"

"Then, I think you have no choice so let's get to work on doing just that. Changing your response. Changing the thought patterns in your consciousness.

"Think along with me about what I am saying as I give you a treatment now, then every day treat yourself somewhat along the same line:

"There is one Infinite Intelligence, one Absolute Mind, and that Mind is in me, through me, as me. So I use that Mind and Its limitless possibilities to create perfect health for myself, right here and right now.

"Any patterns of hate, resentment or anger in me I repudiate, wipe out of my consciousness. And I deny that I have any fever in my body and any thought patterns in my mind to cause fever.

"As a manifestation of Infinite Intelligence I am unique and of worth and I assert that I have the right to express that uniqueness and worth, consistent with the right of others to express their uniqueness and worth. No one dominates me and I dominate no one. As a manifestation of Infinite Intelligence I am love for It is love and I respond to others only with love. Therefore there is nothing in me to create illness.

"I am total health.

"I release this treatment to the Law. The Law accepts it. The Law works on it. The Law produces its results in my life. And so it is."

Within a few weeks Mrs. Marston and her mother-in-law were establishing a new relationship. Mrs. Marston did not find asserting herself easy but she persisted in trying. Her mother-in-law did not stop dominating easily but she began making an attempt.

At any rate Mrs. Marston was able to change her response to the whole situation so that in time the fever disappeared from her body.

CHAPTER X

A Word or Two Can Reveal

a Disease Pattern

Solving health problems, of course, opens the way to improvement in all the other areas of life. For the areas are interrelated. If one's health is improved, one may be better able to use one's talents, so one's financial situation is likely to brighten. If one's fundamental needs for love and affection are satisfactorily met, then one's health is liable to improve. Thus, success in one area automatically lays the groundwork for progress and eventual success in another.

In fact, solving any problem generally helps to solve others. It builds our confidence and usually shows us convincingly how mind can get rid of a problem as well as create it.

The 'parent' thought that produced the 'offspring' of constant fevers in Mrs. Marston revealed itself readily through her chance remark about her mother-in-law. But — except in one instance, that of Julie — I found no more difficulty in discovering the mental equivalents back of the illnesses in any of the case histories that follow. And although I have chosen these particular examples to present to you, I might have chosen any number of others in which the parent-thought for offspring-result was equally apparent.

A Word or Two Can Reveal a Disease Pattern

Stanley Isaac, a tall, slender, high-strung young man who came to me for a problem of asthma, was a hairdresser.

In the course of telling me about himself he assured me that he liked hair dressing well enough and was fairly good at originating new styles to suit his customers. Good enough, I gathered, so that he had a large following at the salon where he worked, a following who would not think of allowing anyone except 'dear Mr. Stanley' to touch their hair.

The only trouble was that 'dear Mr. Stanley', due to increasingly severe attacks of asthma, had recently been forced to call in sick at the salon so often that he feared his employer might be about to fire him.

"She's a real bitch," he told me in a confidential tone, "and it's not that I'm afraid that I can't get another job. I know I can. But it's such a nuisance changing and anyway they're all alike really, aren't they?"

"Who?" I asked, confused.

"Oh, you know, the salons, the women who run them and the ones who come to have their hair done."

I wasn't quite sure what all this had to do with his attacks of asthma so I kept him talking. "Aren't there a number of shops owned or run by men?" I asked. "Why don't you try getting a job in one of them?"

"I could," he answered. "In fact, I have. I worked for a man in a job I had before this one. But it was the same old story. I have a gift for it, I guess."

What he left unsaid made him rather arduous to follow.

"You've a gift for what?" I probed.

He seemed surprised at my inability to understand his vague speech. "Why, for being victimized," he explained, as if to a child.

"Oh," I said.

"Yes," he went on. "It's a pattern that goes through my whole life. I've had four years of psychoanalysis and at least I learned that much. I'm always being victimized. My mother and father started it and everybody I meet just seems to continue what they started. I suppose you could say I ask for it.

Because it's all I know. I've been told that."

"Precisely what do you mean when you say 'victimized'?" I asked.

"Oh, taken advantage of. Misused. Disregarded. Put upon. Ignored. Not considered. I suppose I work harder than anyone else in the salon. But do I get credit for it? Not so you'd notice it. The more I do, the more I'm expected to do. It's always like that with me. Everybody victimizes me."

Indeed, I thought. "Where do you live?" I said aloud. "Are you a native New Yorker?"

"I was born in Brooklyn. I live in Manhattan now."

"With your parents? Alone? Or are you married?"

"With my mother and father. I mean, I used to. My mother died two years ago and my father about a year ago."

"Well, at least they're two people who are no longer victimizing you," I said. "Your mother and father."

An odd expression crossed his face. I couldn't tell whether he was outraged or hurt at my bluntness. He didn't speak for a moment. When he did, his voice was high and unsteady. "You see," he declared, "now you're doing it too."

"Victimizing you, you mean?"

"Yes."

"If so, it's very far from my intention," I answered. "Look, Mr. Isaac, let's say for the moment that you were victimized as a child. By your parents. I don't deny something of the sort is possible. It is. And as a child you would have felt helpless, unable to protect yourself, unable to stand up to those parents, unable to stop them.

"But you're not a child any longer. You are, you tell me, twenty-nine years old. That makes you an adult by anybody's standards. Both your parents are dead so the two one-time strongest authorities in your world are no longer around. There is absolutely no reason I can see why you should continue either to feel or to let yourself be victimized by anybody. There is absolutely no reason I can see why, now that you're an adult, you don't insist on being your own authority in your world. Why you don't stand up and make people stop taking advantage of you, if indeed they are, as you say they are."

"Well, I .... It isn't as easy as you think. It's all very well to talk but when you've always been victimized as I have, you can't ...."

"Yes, you can," I interrupted. "Mr. Isaac, it appears to me that you are more brain-washed than actually victimized. Brain-washed about being victimized. I don't know why you're so convinced or who convinced you. Nor does it matter. I do know if you don't stop thinking of yourself as a victim you are never going to be treated any other way. You'll never change your outer experience until you change the inner patterns in your mind that are creating that experience."

He was now sitting erect and very stiff in his chair. His manner was equally stiff as he said, "Mr. Pace, I came to you for help for my asthma. Not for a lecture on what's wrong with my character."

He started to rise but I restrained him with a gesture.

"Believe me, Mr. Isaac, I am trying to give you help for your asthma. I don't want to insult you. I don't want to tell you what's 'wrong' with your character. I hope and I believe that I have long ceased to think in terms of what's wrong with a person's character but rather in terms of what's wrong with the way he's thinking. Because what's wrong with the way he's thinking is causing whatever troubles or difficulties he may be experiencing."

His tense face did not relax but he remained seated.

"I don't know how much you know about psychosomatic medicine, Mr. Isaac," I went on. "It's that branch of medicine which attempts to discover and deal with any emotional cause that might be back of a physiological disease."

He shook his head, indicating either that he knew very little or nothing at all about the subject. I couldn't tell with him so I decided to assume he knew nothing. "Psychosomatic medicine believes that for many asthmatics an asthma attack may be a substitute for weeping, that the choking, wheezing, gasping and watering of the eyes associated with such an attack may all be symptoms of suppressed crying."

He moved restlessly, in what I interpreted to be protest but which I soon learned was his way of handling an uncomfortable recognition of truth.

"As the authority in your life, Mr. Isaac," I assured him, "you don't have to accept the theory. And, in your case, it may not be correct. But you will have no way of being sure about that unless you at least consider it."

"It's not that," he answered, again moving restlessly. "I am considering it. I've already considered it. Even as you were speaking. Because I did feel" — he put his hand to his chest — "a kind of realization — well, there does seem to be a rightness about what you've been saying. I don't know how to word it any better. But that's how I feel so often when I think someone's been victimizing me. Like crying. But inside. I'd never cry outside, of course. It's inside and it hurts sometimes like a physical wound. But it isn't — isn't a physical wound. And I feel helpless to make it go away."

"You're not helpless, Mr. Isaac. Not at all. The feeling of helplessness goes back to your childhood when you actually may have been helpless. It's a reaction left over from that time. And your wanting to cry is also a reaction from the past. But you can get rid of them both, if you accept the fact that they're only thought patterns in your mind, applicable perhaps to situations in the past but totally inapplicable to any situation in the present.

"And when you do rout them out of your consciousness, I venture to predict you will also have routed out your asthma attacks."

"It's hard to believe . . . ."

"Life is always in the eternal now, Mr. Isaac. The only place any pattern reoccurs is in consciousness. It never reoccurs in the world of form. In the world of form there is no cycle of reoccurrence. It is only in one's consciousness that one can play the same old tape over and over again. But there is nothing your consciousness still needs to understand or dwell upon about the past. You can't change the facts of it. And as a form it is over and gone and can never return.

"Helplessness and the need to cry, Mr. Isaac, are not reality emotions for your world of today. You are an adult man, capable of dealing with other adults on an adult level, on a level where neither you nor they are victim or victimizer."

"You make it sound almost possible," he said.

"It is possible. Now, I'm going to give you a treatment to neutralize and negate these past, out-moded emotions and to replace them with new, today emotions of security, confidence and balance; a treatment for your knowing that Infinite Intelligence is in all, through all, as all; so there is no inferiority and no superiority, no powerful and no helpless, no master and no slave, no victim and no victimizer. Because there is only the One, of which each is a necessary, needed part. Because to that One there is no big and no small, no lesser and no greater, nothing and nobody of lesser or of greater value; each person is of equal value because he was created by the One to be part of the Whole."

I then proceeded to give him the treatment. Afterward, as he was leaving, I reminded him to treat himself similarly daily for as long as he felt the need.

Today — it must be about two years since I first saw him — he is himself the owner of a large hair dressing salon and has at least ten people in his employ. The pattern of victim and victimizer is gone from his consciousness. And the last time we met he told me that he hadn't had an attack of asthma for so long that he considered himself cured.

'But suppose one knew nothing about psychosomatic medicine,' I can hear some of you object, 'I doubt it would have been so easy then to discover the mental equivalent of Mr. Isaac's asthma — his pattern of suppressed weeping.'

My answer to that objection is, first, there are books on psychosomatic medicine, perhaps the most notable being "Mind and Body" by Flanders Dunbar, M.D.; and second, even without knowing anything about psychosomatic medicine Mr. Isaac could, I believe, have tracked down the causes behind his illness on his own.

The clues were evident, if you stop to think about it.

If Mr. Isaac had simply known that illness and disease in the physical body are largely the result of negative, morbid and unhealthy patterns of thought in the mind (which it is one of the purposes of this book to teach people) he could have gone about examining his consciousness for such patterns. Eventually, I feel sure, he would have realized how frequently his thoughts were of being victimized (after all, it was he himself who told me that he had a gift for being victimized) and that these thoughts were just as frequently accompanied by an emotion — a very conscious emotion, you will remember — of wanting to cry, which, however, as he said, he did not permit himself to do.

Yes, if Mr. Isaac had known nothing about psychosomatic medicine but had searched out these two unhealthy patterns in his consciousness, he could have treated himself against them, at the same time treating himself for whatever positive emotions and thought patterns appeared to him to be their opposites and he would have ended up with much the same treatment I gave him. Oh, the words might well have been different but the ideas back of them would have been the same or near enough. And that's what's important.

Because, as I've said, treatment doesn't have to and, indeed, shouldn't take any set form. Its aim is to change negative patterns of causation, to counteract old, harmful, inadequate ways of thinking, to render inoperable the causes of which illness, poverty, bad relationships or failure are the result and to put in their place, fresh, new, creative patterns of health, love, life, peace, supply, success, accomplishment and self-fulfillment.

Let's take one more example in which the mental equivalent was revealed through the words the person used to describe how he felt about the circumstances of his life.

The case came to me through one of my Monday noon meetings. At these meetings students are allowed to ask for answers to questions or for treatments for personal problems, by means of notes which they leave at the desk at the back of the room and which, just before the meeting begins, are brought to me. I read the notes aloud and then answer the questions or give the treatments requested.

Larry's note was so negative (at the time I didn't know to whom the note belonged; students don't sign their names unless they care to) that I found myself stopping in the midst of it to remonstrate, feeling the need, even as I read, to counteract its strong atmosphere of depression, pessimism, self-pity and worthlessness.

" 'When I leave here,' " the note began, " 'I go for financial assistance to a place where in the past I have met with indifference, followed by prejudice and extreme resistance on the part of sadistic, angry clerks who express open delight at my vulnerable, helpless position.' "

"Now, I'm sorry," I interrupted myself, "you sound very masochistic. I cannot imagine that, in the entire place you're talking about, every clerk you meet has these qualities and expresses them toward you, not unless you are consciously or unconsciously asking for that kind of treatment. Bringing such qualities out in them. You must be taking an attitude with you which, without your knowing, forces the people you meet there to treat you as you describe. To treat you as you're expecting to be treated.

"Let me tell you a little story," I continued. "It's about a young man I once met who gave me an account about his study of Zen in Japan. He was of small stature, this young man, wiry, with blond hair. He was a very sensitive, serious-looking young man. About twenty-five or twenty-six. At nineteen he'd decided that he wanted to study Zen and somebody told him of a great master of that teaching in Japan. He made up his mind to work and save his money and go there and study under this great teacher. He didn't say what he worked at or how long it took him to save the money and I didn't ask. Anyway he did get to Japan and was accepted by the master.

"His first instructions were that at the beginning he would be expected to make the fire three times a day on which the Zen master's food would be cooked.

"He made no objection. He supposed he was undergoing

113

a short trial period before his spiritual work was begun. But whenever he made the fire the roshi or Zen master would tell him that he'd made it very badly and would show him how it should have been made. The only trouble was that when he made the fire again, following the new instructions, he would again be told that he'd done a bad job and would be shown yet another way.

"He kept trying but it seemed that no matter how carefully he watched and how closely he followed the changing instructions he was never able to please the master.

"And the master didn't confine his displeasure to looks. He openly criticized, jeered and eventually became verbally abusive toward the young student.

"This went on for about a month. The young man kept trying but he was beginning to wonder why he was never given any spiritual lessons. Finally, when two weeks later he was still just making the fire, he decided that he had wasted his money coming, that he wasn't going to be taught anything and that he therefore had better leave and go home, though he was bitterly disappointed.

"He made his resolution one night just before he fell asleep but he told himself that he would wait until the following evening before informing the master of his intention. The next morning he made the fire as usual and as usual when he was finished the master again began to criticize his work, calling him lazy, stupid, inept and a number of other equally insulting things.

"The boy bowed his head in acceptance as he'd done ever since his arrival. But unexpectedly the master, perhaps sensing his dissatisfaction, picked up a broom and began beating him over the head and shoulder. Finally, the boy told me, he could take no more and he reached out and grabbed the master's kimono and was just about to say, 'Listen, you, you are to stop calling me names and beating me with that broom or I am going to break you in two.'

"But he never got the words out because when he had grabbed the master's kimono, he had also raised his head and now he was looking into the master's eyes and suddenly he knew that he had been taught and had learned his first spiritual lesson.

"And the lesson was that as long as you think of yourself as lazy, stupid or inept or allow someone else to convince you that that's what you are, then that's the way you're going to be treated.

"And you who wrote this note — when you stand up and say to yourself, 'It's absolutely not true that I'm vulnerable or helpless. It's absolutely not true that I'm the kind of person who encounters indifference, prejudice or resistance,' then nobody will treat you the way you describe on this piece of paper.

"These words you write are full of unpleasant emotions, full of negativism. You will, indeed, have unpleasant experiences as long as you carry such emotions with you. 'Who express open delight at my vulnerable, helpless position.' No, you must stop thinking this way. You are not vulnerable or helpless and you must stop thinking of yourself as such.

"Look, haven't you heard me say that we are all surrounded by an atmosphere created by our thoughts, an atmosphere that works like a magnet? It attracts or repels experiences according to its make-up. If you do continue to think of yourself as vulnerable and helpless and the type of person who always meets with indifference, prejudice and resistance, then you are, in fact, going to attract into your experience 'sadistic, angry clerks,' as you put it, who will treat you the way you are expecting to be treated."

What I said at that meeting apparently got through to Larry because he came to talk with me later. At that time he filled me in with more details of his situation. He was ill, out of work and, he muttered harshly, 'on charity.'

"I hate it," he said from between clenched teeth. "This having to accept what's doled out to me. Like some beggar. But I can't work. I've got a stomach ulcer. I'm too sick."

"What did you do before you became ill?" I asked. He was middle-aged and I wondered what was in store for him.

115

"Bricklaying. Until I got too weak to heft the bricks all day. But I hated that too. Bricklaying, I mean. What I always wanted was to be an architect. Only there wasn't enough money at home to send me through school. I had to go to work early. Take whatever job I could get.

"My younger brother — he's the architect — got to go to school. Part of the money I brought home went toward his schooling. It eats me up inside every time I think about it. How he got what I wanted. Just because he was younger and my mother's favorite.

"Now he's the big guy and I'm the nothing. All I can do is lie around my apartment all day, trying to rest and not worry and get back my strength like the doctor told me to do."

"Where is your brother?" I asked. "You helped him."

"He's around. Oh sure, I could take his charity, instead of the other. He's willing to support me. Oh-yeah, he's willing. Only I'm not. I don't want anything from him. That would — that would really eat me up inside."

An ulcer (wherever it is, in the stomach or on a leg) is defined, according to the dictionary, as "a sore . . . accompanied by disintegration of tissue." It has the effect of resembling tissue that is being eaten away.

Larry had twice spoken about things that either did or would eat him up inside.

Several times after that day he consulted me in my office and I tried to show him how his attitudes were affecting his body but he wasn't an easy case. His feelings of worthlessness, vulnerability, helplessness, bitterness and self-pity went deep and he was unwilling to grapple with them to any great extent. And with the reality always before him of his brother, who was all that he himself wanted to be and wasn't, he was not able readily to change his self-image.

He did make some improvement, however. To the point where he was at least able to return to work, get off the hated charity and away from the clerks, who, incidentally, he had come to see, were often more harried and over-worked than angry, sadistic, indifferent and resistant.

116

CHAPTER XI

Nature's Healing Processes

Can Be Greatly Speeded Up

I don't care how a cure of illness, disease or injury comes about. If a person has a broken leg and I do a treatment that he or she is free of pain, that the leg heals quickly and is again perfect I do not believe that these things must come about in some miraculous way, without benefit of the medical profession. I know, of course, that they can but I am not concerned that they do. For, to me, cures achieved by the medical profession are just as valuable, just as miraculous, just as much the action of Infinite Intelligence as those that seemingly come about by themselves.

I am not so much interested in defying the laws of Nature as I am in complying with them, at the level of our present human-race mind consciousness.

But even in cases where I know that treatment is very probably only going to assist in the cure, I endeavor to determine the mental equivalent back of the resulting disability. Knowing what predisposed one to injury, catching a disease or falling ill identifies the subconscious pattern that needs changing. And working to change that pattern can, I believe, speed the cure, can accelerate the process of getting rid of what I often call the 'tail-end of the experience' — the recovery period.

Two cases in my practice stand out as illustrations of this point, the cases of Wanda and Julie, both of whom had speedy recoveries when the mental equivalents that had caused their problems were discovered.

When I mentioned a broken leg I had in mind the specific case of Wanda Morrison, one of my former students. She slipped on the ice and fell one winter day during a driving sleet storm.

She had been hurrying to open up her place of business, a small dry-goods store which she had run alone since her husband's death ten years previously.

The break in the leg was a bad one and Wanda was taken to a nearby hospital where she was told she would have to have an operation. She would not consent and insisted on phoning me.

"Wanda," I told her, "my advice to you is to follow your doctor's orders. If I fell and broke my leg I can assure you I'd rejoice there's a doctor who knows how to set bones. I wouldn't wait around, treating that Infinite Intelligence sets the bones. Intellectually I believe anything is possible and intellectually I believe that the Infinite Intelligence is the totality of possibilities. But I also know It has to acomplish those possibilities through me. I know that I can objectify only what I can comprehend. I can't objectify beyond my understanding. And at my present stage of development I can't expand my consciousness to where I can believe that a broken leg, with the bones out of place, can be healed without the help of a physician. Can you?"

"But I can't have an operation," Wanda said, between sobs. "I've got to keep the store open. I need the money. For myself and Sondra (Sondra is her daughter). I can't afford six weeks in the hospital and then four months hobbling around in a cast."

"Look, Wanda, you and I know it doesn't have to be six weeks in the hospital and four months hobbling around on crutches, no matter what they say there. We know we can speed up the time of healing at least. You have that operation and I'll treat that it's a complete success, that the bones knit quickly and perfectly and that you're up, out of the hospital and back in the store so fast those doctors will have to shake their heads at your remarkable recovery."

"Oh, Eric, what am I going to do? Why did it have to happen? Why did it have to happen to me?" Her sobs increased.

"Wanda," I ordered, "stop it. Crying isn't going to help. All right, why did it happen to you? Think about it. Find the pattern. It's too late now to prevent the accident but a consciousness that no longer has that particular negative isn't going to be interested in prolonging your trouble."

"Find the pattern!" Wanda exclaimed. "I don't have to look very far. I know it. Ever since I can remember, my mother — whenever I've had to go out on a day like today — she's never failed to remind me, 'Now you be careful, Wanda. It's icy out. Watch your step. If you don't you'll fall and break a leg.'

"Icy. Fall. Break a leg. What could be clearer?"

"All right. Don't dwell on it," I said. "We'll begin to treat it out of your consciousness here and now. So it won't cause you any further difficulties."

"But, Eric, it could be five months!"

"Wanda, you are going to cooperate with the doctor. You are not going to concentrate on five months but on five weeks. You are going to concentrate on being the best patient the doctor's ever had, the most cooperative, fastest healing patient who ever got a broken leg. Right? Then it won't be five months. You'll be back in that store of yours before you know it."

And within six weeks she was not only out of the hospital as the doctor had told her she would be, she was back in her store, driving her car, doing everything she'd been doing before the accident, except that she was on crutches.

She was even coming to the Center at her regular time,

to sell books at the book counter, hobbling up the long flight of stairs.

Those of us who would see her coming had to steel ourselves from helping her or from giving her sympathy and special attention because of the cast and the crutch. But I had admonished everybody, including myself, "Don't commiserate with Wanda because she's been injured. Don't fuss over her. Fuss over her, if you have to fuss at all, because she's here with the rest of us, doing her work as usual. Ignore her handicap as much as possible. Talk to her about other things. Keep her mind off it."

In a week we'd all practically forgotten Wanda's crutch. But Wanda hadn't. We were having a banquet at the Center in less than three weeks and Wanda was determined to be free of the crutch by that time, to walk into the banquet hall without it.

She did too. When I met her that day she said to me, "See, Eric!" and motioned toward her feet.

I looked down at them, puzzled. "What? New shoes?"

"No. Oh, you didn't even notice. No crutches! Not even a cane."

"How long?" I asked. "How long has it been in all?"

"Just about nine weeks and it hasn't even seemed that long."

The negative causation back of Wanda's injury was evident even to Wanda herself and it became evident with almost no digging in each of the other instances I've presented. But now and then I come across a case like Julie's, in which I work for weeks and sometimes worry that I'm never going to get a hint.

Julie came to me after doctors at one of the city's leading hospitals had diagnosed her trouble as cancer of the throat. Julie didn't believe in doctors or hospitals, an attitude she'd acquired from both her parents. On her own she'd never have gone to one but had consented after much pleading by her frantic husband.

The diagnosis stunned them both.

Six cobalt treatments were recommended by the doctor, before hospitalization and surgery.

The husband seemed to freeze with fear of losing her but Julie rallied her forces, started with the cobalt treatments and then came to me.

Now, Science of Mind believes that back of many manifestations of cancer there is a pattern of secrecy in the patient's consciousness. By that I mean that the individual is harboring some secret in his or her consciousness. And it must not just be any secret; it must be a secret that causes guilt, along with an unwillingness or inability to share it with anybody.

I explained this belief and waited for Julie's reaction.

She seemed to have no reaction and she told me calmly that she had no secret of that kind that she knew of.

Since I lacked a possible mental equivalent, my treatments for her had to be simple denials that there were any patterns in her consciousness that could cause cancer, plus affirmations that she was free of all symptoms of illness and that she demonstrated only perfect health and wholeness.

At the end of the six cobalt treatments the doctors informed Julie and her husband with amazement that the cancer was 90 per cent gone. But they were cautious; they could not, they warned, predict its future course. Still, in view of her extraordinary progress, she would be allowed a month free of treatment. But then she would have to return for hospitalization, further tests and evaluation.

Meanwhile, whenever Julie came for her appointment with me, I would again bring up the matter of secrets.

Her answer was always the same. She had no secret she felt guilty about. She had no secret, period.

The month passed and Julie went back to her doctor. The cancer in her throat appeared at a standstill but the doctor nevertheless began immediate arrangements for her to be hospitalized. A bed, however, proved unavailable until the last of that week so Julie was able to come to me for one more time.

I sensed a difference in her from the moment she entered my office. I couldn't put my finger on what it was, except that she was more subdued and seemed to have something she wanted to say but couldn't. We talked for awhile about her response to the disappointment (she had been sure that all trace of the cancer would be gone) and I kept sensing this wanting to talk but holding back in her.

Not until I said, "All right, Julie, let's quiet our minds and treat again," did she suddenly blurt out:

"I didn't think I'd have to come to it but I guess I was wrong. I do have what I guess you could call a secret. I'd never have called it that — exactly — but maybe that's what it is. And I do feel guilty about it. Not in the way you might think but in another way. If we'd told everybody from the start it would have been sheer hell for us but at least maybe I'd also have had the courage to . . . . Oh, it doesn't matter. It's too late now."

"I think it does matter," I said. "It may matter very much. Tell me about it."

"Telling you isn't going to relieve the guilt. It's too late for that. Too late to change anything. Too late to give him children. We're both too old."

"Well, if we can't relieve all the guilt — and I still think we can — maybe we can relieve part of it. Tell me anyhow. When it's no longer a secret some of the guilt is automatically gone."

"Basil is black," she said.

For a moment I didn't comprehend what she was saying. I knew her husband Basil. He was dark, in contrast to her fairness, but I had not known he was black. And, of course, it wouldn't have mattered to me if I had, as it doesn't matter to many people of my generation and younger.

But she and Basil were nearly sixty years old and abruptly I realized that at the time they were married, a union between a black man and a white woman could have mattered very much indeed.

"Basil is black," she repeated and now she appeared to

savor the words as if she were glad to be saying them. "I knew it before I fell in love with him. He told me. But I couldn't help myself. I loved him from the first time, the moment he touched me, touched my hand. I still do. So much that I was willing to marry him, whatever the cost. Willing to run away from home — my parents would have disowned me anyhow—and go some place where nobody would know us.

"He was willing too but he told me that maybe we ought to think about it. I said I didn't have to think about it. I wanted to marry him. He said that wasn't what he meant about thinking about it. What he meant was that maybe we wouldn't have to run away. Because he didn't have any family. He was just up from the south. Nobody in the city knew him. It was a big city. Easy to get lost in. So he wasn't likely ever to meet anybody who'd known him from the small town he'd come from.

"He'd told me he was black, he said, because he loved me and felt he had to be honest with me. He hadn't told anybody else though and why did anybody else have to know? He'd been other places, other cities, frequently passed for white, without anyone suspecting. Why couldn't he just start passing as white permanently? If we didn't tell anyone my parents would accept him, we could get married, stay right here and be happy.

"We discussed whether it would work, for weeks. We were alternately sure and not sure. We would kiss and cling to each other in hope and weep in each others' arms in doubt. But finally we decided we had to take the chance. We loved each other too much not to.

"So Basil went to my father and asked if we could marry. My father and my mother were delighted. They loved Basil too. My father's dead now. He never knew. My mother's still alive but she doesn't know either, of course, and Basil would never consider telling her. She adores him and is so proud of him. He spoils her.

"We've lived a lie for nearly forty years. Perhaps it

wouldn't matter much now if we did tell the truth. To a lot of people anyhow. But I don't suppose there's much point in it either. We're too old to start disrupting our life at this point. When the damage has already been done."

"Damage?" I asked.

"The damage of my letting him sacrifice for me."

"His identity, you mean? But you didn't just 'let' him, I gather from what you've told me. It was his choice, as much if not more than yours, wasn't it?"

"Not his identity. That may be a word for other people but it's not a word for Basil. Basil's sure of his identity. Inside. Where it counts. No, not his identity. But we didn't have children. I never insisted. I guess I was afraid one of them might turn out so black no one could mistake it for anything but the child of a black man."

"Did Basil want children?"

"He never said so but he must have."

"Why don't you ask him? Why don't you tell him how you feel, your fears, your guilt?"

"What good would it do? If he did want children and didn't urge me, I'd only feel worse, more guilty."

"I don't see how you could feel more guilty than you apparently do. You've felt guilty enough to have made yourself pretty ill. And just suppose he didn't want them. Just suppose he's been completely happy with the life you both chose? He looks happy when he isn't worrying about you."

She was beginning to hope. "Maybe I will," she said.

The following week Julie went into the hospital and it was Basil who came to see me.

"Julie told me what she's been worrying about, Eric," he said as we shook hands. "And I hope I've been able to reassure her. Because the truth is I've never considered I sacrificed anything for her. I've always considered myself a darn lucky man to get her. She was the one woman for me. She's made me completely happy. I look back on our life and I wouldn't change it for anything.

"I knew what I was doing when I suggested I pass for white. I'm a strong character when it comes to things like that. In a different time, in a different place, I might have made a different decision. If we were kids today . . . . But people are born when they're born. They have to make the best they can of their circumstances.

"Anyway I never wanted children for the same reason Julie didn't. Though I thought I was the one depriving her. I never realized she might think she was depriving me. I didn't feel any deprivation. I had made my choice. Julie and Julie's happiness were all I wanted.

"It's all I still want. And if anything happens to her, for me, there's nothing."

He lowered his head and I could see that he was struggling to keep from breaking.

"We've got things going for us now, Basil," I told him. "She's gotten the guilt out. She loves you too. Very much. And if you've been able to assure her that she hasn't hurt you and that you love her too — well, it's a lot for a woman to live for."

"If she does get better — well, there is one thing I've wanted. I've always wanted to go back to a warmer climate. I don't think Julie would mind getting away from the weather here either. We could pack her mother up and take her along with us."

"Not 'if' she gets better, Basil, 'when' she gets better."

Tears sprang to his eyes. "Yeah, you're right. When she gets better, then I'm going to talk to her about getting away from here. So I'll be wanting you to treat for us to find the right place and for a part-time job for me. To supplement our income until I'm sixty-five."

Julie had two more cobalt treatments. By the end of the second treatment, the cancer in her throat was completely gone and it has not returned to this day.

Three months after she was discharged by her doctor Julie and Basil and her mother moved to Hawaii. Basil works in a stationery store there.

Perhaps you too have a health problem, like Julie and Wanda and Larry and Stanley and the others — including me — once had. Since I can't know what it is specifically, I am going to give, at this point, a general treatment for health which is worded so that, if you care to, you can make it your own:

I know that there is one Power and that Power is perfect. I know that that Power created me in order to express in me, through me and as me. Therefore I know that It functions in me as perfect health, right here and right now.

I negate and nullify all negative, unhealthy and morbid patterns in my consciousness that hinder, delay or obstruct the appearance of my good which is vibrant, dynamic, radiant health.

I know that health is the state of my body right here and right now, always has been and always will be.

I release this treatment into the Law, knowing the Law does the work and demonstrates it in my life. And so it is.

CHAPTER XII

Acquiring a Receptive Attitude

Toward Money

Money enough for our needs, ease in finances, not only frees us from want and worry but from the niggardly existence of 'do without' and 'make do.'

Life is obviously limited for anyone who suffers from ill health. But it is also limited, though perhaps less obviously, for those who lack enough money to enjoy not only the necessities but the pleasures, amenities and beautiful things the world has to offer, seemingly in such abundance for some, while at the same time in such meagerness for others.

Sometimes I think there are more ambiguous feelings about money than about any other entity in our culture. The Havenots want but feel guilty about wanting. The Haves often feel guilty about having. The Havenots tend to envy but also to have a feeling of superior virtue. The Haves may not feel superior but they frequently tend to view the Havenots as objects of pity, compassion or charity (occasionally of scorn).

Many people even avoid using the word 'money' because it makes them feel uncomfortable, almost as though the very concept contained within it an idea of something shameful —

greed, evil, corruption, ruthlessness, shady dealings.

But money has no such qualities in itself. The qualities are in the people who misuse money.

Money itself is as much a creation of the Infinite Intelligence, acting through Man, as is a flower, a child, a tree or the song of a bird.

Money is not a handful of coins or bills, a paycheck, a bankbook with a deposit of six figures, real estate or a boxful of jewels. Money is merely a means of exchange for ideas, goods and services.

There is absolutely nothing wrong with money per se. But try telling some people that. Is there anything wrong with a coca cola bottle? Not if it's used to hold coca cola. Not unless it's misused as a weapon to hit someone over the head. Is there anything wrong with certain drugs per se? Not when they're used by the medical profession to alleviate pain and suffering or to bring about a cure. Not unless they're misused as uppers or downers or as a means of escaping life by blotting out consciousness.

If Infinite Intelligence is everywhere, in all, through all and as all, It is in money just as much as It is in the greatest saint, the most beautiful rose, the cutest baby or the most exquisite sunset.

But the human race has many deep-seated misconceptions about money, buried in the psyche, garnered from books, from stories, fables, myths, from sayings passed on from one generation to another:

'The love of money is the root of all evil.' 'Poverty is a virtue.' 'Money is hard to come by honestly.' 'It is easier for a camel to go through the eye of a needle than for a rich man to enter into the kingdom of God.' 'For money he would sell his own soul.' 'Be not greedy of filthy lucre.'

To me, these are old, out-moded ways of thinking that are responsible for much of the lack, limitation and misery in which many people live.

The love of money is not the root of all evil. If anything is the root of all evil — and I myself do not think in terms of evil but of incorrect choices — then evil thoughts are for they are the roots of so-called evil results.

Poverty is not a virtue. Poverty is an unenlightened state of mind that refuses to allow itself to expect and accept the abundance of the universe, created for the use of all, that feels guilty at wanting and unworthy of having. Does one feel guilty for wanting or having a flower? No, one handles it carefully, cares for it and cherishes it as long as it lives and even when it dies one tosses it away gently because after all it's still a flower.

But the coins and paper money are no less the manifestation of Absolute Mind, First Cause, the all-knowing, all-giving Creator than a flower.

Each serves its unique purpose. When you need money a flower will not do. You can't go into a butchershop and say, I want a roast, and give the butcher a gladiola in return. Oh, of course, you can but he's not going to give you the roast. And you can't go to a hospital to visit a sick friend and take him a five dollar bill. Oh, of course, you can but he's going to be embarrassed and think you're a little crazy. You bring him flowers because you know their color and form and beauty will cheer him.

If you are hungry a five dollar bill is not going to get you food if there's no place for you to buy food. You can't satisfy your hunger by eating the five dollar bill any more than by eating the flower. Everything has its purpose. And money is no different from anything else. So, if you need it and want it, you had better start changing your consciousness from one that fears, despises, feels unworthy or disapproves of money to one that welcomes, respects, loves, feels worthy of and approves of it.

Actually, of course, prosperity doesn't only consist of having money. Prosperity is the ability to feel free in the world of form, to feel at ease and comfortable on the material plane of life. Prosperity is the ability to do or have what you want to do or have at the moment you want to do or have it. For one person that might be to take a bicycle ride through

Central Park. For another it might mean flying to Palma de Mallorca to stretch out on the beach in the sun or to do some scuba diving. The amount of money needed in each case would vary greatly. Yet if each person were truly doing what he or she wanted to do at that moment both would be equally prosperous.

So when you treat yourself (give yourself a treatment) for prosperity, remember that money is only a part of prosperity. Concentrate on having whatever you think you need to feel free and prosperous, to have and do the things you want, to be able to choose the experiences you find the most satisfying, the most fulfilling.

And don't decide you want something just to keep up with the Joneses. Whatever you treat for, make sure that you really want it for itself. Not just because others have it.

But, to be realistic, for most of us in our culture, prosperity does mean money, enough money to satisfy our needs and wants, though that's simply because money is, as I've said, our means of exchange for ideas, goods and services.

So okay — how do you change a poverty consciousness into a money or prosperity consciousness? Well, first, of course, you avail yourself of the use of the technique of treatment but I'd prefer to go into that method later and then give you, as an example, a general treatment for prosperity you can use, if you don't yet feel capable of making up one of your own.

Second, you memorize a few positive sayings about money and say them to yourself, to counteract the negative ones you may have either consciously or unconsciously been thinking. Repeat them to yourself several times a day for at least a week. Sayings such as:

"Increased means and increased leisure are the two civilizers of man." (Benjamin Disraeli)

"There is nothing so degrading as the constant anxiety about one's means of livelihood . . . . Money is like a sixth sense without which you cannot make a complete use of the other five." (William Somerset Maugham)

"Poverty is the parent of revolution and crime." (Aristotle)

"Money, which represents the prose of life, and which is hardly spoken of in parlors without an apology, is, in its effects and laws, as beautiful as roses." (Ralph Waldo Emerson)

"The world is his who has money to go over it." (Also Ralph Waldo Emerson).

Remember now, I am not suggesting that you teach yourself to be greedy or grasping or dishonest or callous of another's right to his good or prosperity. Science of Mind always emphasizes that anything you want, money along with other things, must be acquired consistent with good for everyone. What I am saying is that to acquire your share of the abundance of the universe you must have a consciousness that accepts money as a commodity that can be used for good, just as easily as it can be used for the so-called evil purposes so many of us have been taught are its true benefits.

So don't be grim about your quotations. The old sayings have enough of grimness in them. Put a little fun in the ones you use to counteract them. Laughter is an effective antidote for the grim.

Henry Louis Mencken's "Poverty is a soft pedal upon all branches of human activity, not excepting the spiritual," is good for setting the mind straight.

And then there's Franklin Pierce Adams's amusing rhyme, contrasting himself and a rich man. The rich man, he says, has a limousine, townhouse and country estate. He puffs a $2 cigar—Adams said 50 cents (pre-inflation price)—while he "jeers at Fate." He himself, Adams complains, has to grub for a living. Would he change places? he asks. The answer to his own question is a resounding, "You bet I would!"

You might also learn some sayings of Ernest Holmes. You can memorize them and repeat them to yourself, type them and read them over or record them on a tape recorder and play them several times a day, until they begin to penetrate your unconscious and oust any belief in lack and limitation:

"We see abundance in the Universe. We cannot count the grains of sand on a single beach. The earth contains untold riches and the very air is vibrant with power. Why, then, is man weak, poor and afraid?"

"The storehouse of Nature may be filled with good, but the good is locked up to the ignorant. When we learn to trust the Universe, we shall be happy, prosperous and well. We must learn to come under that Divine Government and accept the fact that Nature's table is ever filled. Never was there a Cosmic failure."

Now, I must confess that if you go looking for proverbs, quotations and sayings about money (or prosperity or wealth) you are going to find that there are many more which deprecate it than otherwise. Remind yourself that that's because they're mostly all concerned with the human-race misconceptions about money, stemming from its misuse. You are changing your consciousness about money, not as something to misuse but as something to make life freer, more pleasant, more comfortable and more beautiful.

Another thing to remind yourself of in changing your consciousness is that hoarding money is a commitment to lack and limitation. There is a difference between sensible saving and hoarding. When we think of increasing the supply in the universe that is always at our disposal, we have to realize that it increases the more we accept the idea that its nature is one of constant circulation, one of constant flowing in and flowing out. It comes to us, we accept it, we use it and then we release it. We never exhaust the reserves the universe has for us so there is no reason to hoard.

Always depend on the Principle, in money as in everything, depend on the fact that the Absolute Mind is always creating and that It is going to give you what you set into motion through your thought and your emotions. Absolute Mind creates money with the same lavishness that It creates other things but, as a means of exchange, money must be circulated, must be used in order to serve its purpose and when it is serving its purpose it will come back multiplied.

Now I'm not telling you, Be profligate. Throw your money around.

I'm telling you, Don't hoard, use money but use it wisely, with prudence.

A few years ago I worked with a lady who was looking for the right house for herself and her family. She wanted the house to be in a neighborhood that would be both convenient for transportation to schools, stores, and her husband's place of business but one which would also have good, interesting, friendly neighbors.

I asked her in what areas she'd been looking and she told me. Then I asked her if she'd seen anything that came close to being what she thought she was looking for and she replied that she had, that she'd seen several houses that might suit her purposes.

"Oh," I said. "But you can't decide which so you want us to treat that you choose the right one?"

"No." She shook her head. "Anyone would do. There's not all that much difference. But I don't want to pay the prices they're asking. I've checked with the town clerk. Right now he hasn't anything. I was hoping he would. You know, you can get a tremendous bargain if you can get a house through the town clerk because he has a list of the ones somebody has to sell either to settle an estate or because he can't pay his taxes."

Now, this woman and her family have plenty of money. I looked at her. I've known her long enough to tell her the unvarnished truth when I think it's necessary. "You are hoping to profit from someone else's misfortune. You are hoping somebody will die and somebody else will have to sell a house cheap in order to settle an estate, or that somebody will be so down on his luck that he won't be able to pay his taxes. In most people's book, Darlene, that makes you a mean woman."

She was so shocked she nearly fell out of her chair. At first she couldn't speak but finally she gasped, "You're right. How awful! I never thought of it that way."

"Well, you'd better. And not just because it makes you mean by most people's standards. What do you think you're doing to your consciousness? What kind of patterns do you think you're putting into it? You have enough money to buy the house you want. Without going to such extremes of hoarding. Not that you shouldn't be trying to get a fair price. But what you're doing can only harm you in the end. You're thinking lack and limitation when you have plenty. Pretty soon lack and limitation is what you're going to get in place of your plenty."

She didn't need any further lecture. She saw my point only too clearly. Within a week she had chosen and bought one of the houses she had previously seen. She really wasn't a mean woman. She'd gotten mixed up in her thinking but she didn't really want anyone to suffer. And she didn't want such patterns in her subconscious mind. Nor did she want patterns of limitation and lack there, for herself or anyone else.

Bargain hunting isn't inherently bad but it has to be watched that it isn't done as a means of hoarding rather than as a means of prudently using momentarily limited resources.

If you have a certain amount of money to spend this month, that's the amount you have to use. But if your income goes up and you don't begin to expand the amount you use, then you're placing lack and limitation back into your consciousness.

People can also hoard the ideas, goods and services they could and should give to the world in the form of their talents and abilities and thus too stop the circulation of money, into as well as out of their experience.

A good illustration of this point is the poverty-stricken young painter who came to me to help him get what he called 'the Pace prosperity consciousness.'

We worked for several sessions and then one day he came into my office, grinning from ear to ear. "It's working," he practically shouted. "I've got a commission from a guy who wants me to do a painting and he's agreed to pay me

$400." And then quieting down, he said, "My God, Eric, you don't know how I needed this sale. I was just about broke."

"Great!" I exclaimed. "How soon do you expect to get the painting done? How soon can you look forward to being paid?"

"Oh, within the next couple of weeks I'd say. He's not cramping my style. He's not trying to dictate what I paint. He's letting me go ahead and paint whatever I want."

"That is a demonstration."

The following week he was still in high spirits and painting happily. But the week following that he arrived with his chin just about down on his chest.

"What happened?" I questioned him solicitously.

He told me the story in incoherent little bits and pieces. It's pretty incredible but it went something like this:

"Well, he, the guy, came for the painting," he began and stopped.

"Didn't he like it?" I prodded sympathetically.

"Oh, yeah. Sure, he liked it. At least he said he did."

"Well?"

"How could I be sure? Be sure he really liked it, I mean. He got out his checkbook to pay me but I told him, 'No.'

"'But we agreed on $400,' he said.

"'I know,' I acknowledged. 'It's not the $400. But how can I be sure you really like it?'

"'I do,' he answered. 'If I didn't I'd tell you. Ask you to change it in some way.'

"'But you gave me carte blanche,' I reminded him.

"'I know that,' he answered.

"'Then how could you ask me to change anything?'

"'My God, man, I'm not asking you to change anything,' he said.

"'I know,' I admitted. 'That's what makes it so difficult for me to know whether you really like it or not, your giving me carte blanche so now you can't ask me to change anything.'

"'But I really don't want anything changed,' he argued.

135

'I like it. I like it just the way it is. Come on, man, don't be so difficult. I'll give you your check and you wrap up the painting so I can take it home on the subway.'

" 'On the subway!' I cried.

"He looked up from writing out the check. 'Sure on the subway,' he said. 'How else do you expect me to get it home?'

" 'But it's a painting,' I protested. 'I painted it out of my guts. It's an expression of the way I feel about life. It's a work of art. It's part of my very soul.'

" 'What do you want me to do?' he asked. 'Am I supposed to walk it home, carrying it in my arms like a baby?'

" 'No, but . . . . How far is it? It isn't very far. Couldn't you at least take a taxi?' I said. 'I mean, it's a work of art. I created it out of my guts. Suppose something happened to it on the subway?'

" 'You selling me this painting, man, or aren't you?' he demanded. I could see he was beginning to get mad but I didn't care.

" 'Well, I made it for you,' I countered, 'but I can see I can't sell it to you. You don't appreciate it.'

" 'Man,' he told me. 'You are out of your mind.'

" 'Maybe,' I said. 'But I'm still not going to sell it to you.'

" 'Then keep it,' he answered. And when he left he had the nerve to add, 'There are dozens of painters as good if not better than you are. You're out of your mind. You and your work of art.' "

I had listened with increasing amazement. When he finished I said quietly, "Harry, do you really believe you refused to sell your painting because your prospective buyer didn't appreciate it?"

"Well, sure," he answered.

"I think you never wanted to sell that painting in the first place. I think you don't really ever want to sell any of your paintings. That's why you don't often find anybody who wants to buy one. You hoard your painting like a miser hoards money. Because you're afraid that any time your talent is going to run dry and you're not going to be able to paint any more.

"We shouldn't be treating you for money prosperity, Harry. We should be treating you against hoarding your talents and abilities. You're putting lack and limitation on them and you are going to lose them if you continue the way you're going, just like you lost that $400 sale."

It took Harry a long time to break his unconscious pattern of hoarding his talent but he finally did break it. The first evidence was that he gave a painting away — to me. I took it too and not long afterward he sold one and soon he sold another and then he began to sell with some regularity.

His talent for painting shows no sign of declining but rather of growing with each sale. As, of course, so does his prosperity.

CHAPTER XIII

Making Abundance
Happen to You

Many people may be failing to achieve the prosperity they maintain they want — and may actually be trying very hard to acquire — because they don't enjoy the work they're doing. They don't love the work through which they are trying to obtain that prosperity and which they view as their only or principal source of income.

That's a third thing to remember when you're trying to get a prosperity consciousness — you have to love the work you're doing. If indeed a job appears at the moment to be your principal means of obtaining the money you want, then you must love it in order to do your best in it. People don't get raises in jobs they don't love. You must love money for the purpose it serves, in order to attract it to you. You must love your job, in order to attract raises in your paycheck. Anything you love you attract to you. Anything you love you do well at.

So if you do want to be prosperous and don't love your job, then you should either find yourself another job you can love or change your consciousness about your present one.

Andrew Adams was one of those people who don't like

their jobs. He was a space salesman for magazines, hated every minute of his work and was doing very badly in it when one day he happened to walk by the New York Science of Mind headquarters. Something in the display window caught his eye and he found himself dropping into the bookstore and asking what the place was all about. The young man there told him that a lecture had just begun upstairs and that he might go up and listen. It was open to the public.

I happened to be giving the lecture and when it was over Andrew stopped me as I was leaving the hall. He asked if he might make an appointment with me. I gave him one for a week later, on a Tuesday.

He appeared promptly that Tuesday, sat in the chair across the desk from mine — and began to chew his fingernails.

I'm not good at watching a man chew his fingernails and Andrew seemed bent on chewing his down to the quick. So I hurried to get him talking about his problem. It wasn't an unfamiliar one — at least to me. But there were several unusual twists to it.

He had a job. He didn't like it. He wasn't doing well.

So far, only too familiar. But the unusual part wasn't long in coming. He told me where he lived and I recognized the section as one of the wealthiest in Connecticut. He told me that he maintained a large house there for his wife and four children but that he was hundreds of dollars in debt, how many hundreds he didn't have the faintest idea.

"No idea at all?" I murmured.

He shook his head. "All I know is that there's stacks and stacks of bills. In my dresser drawers. I don't even look at them any more when they come. I just stuff them in a drawer, under my socks, my underclothes, my shirts. Anywhere I can still find room."

"Aren't you putting yourself in a pretty dangerous position?" I asked. "Isn't somebody bound to start legal action of some kind soon?"

"Yes." He groaned. "Somebody may already have done

so for all I know. I suppose in time I can lose everything, the cars, the property, the house, even the furniture — everything. And I don't dare think what could happen after that."

"Your wife — how does she feel about all this?"

"She doesn't know. I haven't told her. I mean she knows we're a bit strapped. I couldn't keep that from her. But she doesn't know how bad it is."

"How do you feel about each other? Do you love her? Does she love you?"

"Love her? She's wonderful. I don't deserve her. She's wonderful. Beautiful. Loving. Intelligent. We've been in love since we were teenagers."

"I see. You love her but you don't trust her?" I had to get him to open up more.

"Trust her? Of course I trust her. What has trust to do with it?"

"You're not telling her. That doesn't show much trust. You're setting her up for a tremendous blow. I can only explain that either by the fact that you don't love her or you don't trust her. You don't trust the way she'll react."

"I told you I love her. Don't you understand? That's what makes it so difficult. Worrying about what's going to happen to the house, the cars, everything. About what I'm going to do about taking care of her and the children if we lose everything. Worrying about where we'll live."

"Did you ever stop to think that if she had some idea of the state of affairs, she might be able to help?"

"Help? How? Athena comes from a wealthy family. She's never worked a day in her life."

"Which doesn't mean she can't or at least that she might not have other ideas of ways she could help."

"No. No, I can't tell her. I just can't."

There was such agony in his voice that I didn't press the matter further. I changed the subject to his work, why he didn't like it and what kind of work he thought he might like to do, explaining how important it was to enjoy what one was doing.

I didn't fare much better in this area. He didn't like his job because of the pressure in it. But even if it didn't have any pressure he wouldn't like it anyway. It just didn't interest him. Never had. But as for what he'd enjoy doing — he'd never thought about that much. Didn't have time. He liked singing. In choral groups. But, of course, he knew that wasn't what I meant. No, he just didn't know what he'd like to do and at the moment he was too scared to think of anything except those bills.

I couldn't seem to keep him from going around in circles but after I'd given him a treatment for prosperity and also for his finding a job that would be right for him — one he'd enjoy and in which he could better use his talents and abilities — he appeared more relaxed. He left after asking for another appointment.

Not until five appointments later did he confide to me that he'd finally taken all the bills out of his drawers, gathered them together, was beginning to sort them and to take a look at how bad his situation was.

It was bad, very bad, no mistake about that and yet rather than being more depressed he actually seemed to feel better. He had literally been hiding the gravity of his state, like a child, even from himself. Now he'd taken a step toward facing whatever lay ahead and it was obvious he felt less of a child and more of an adult, and liked himself better.

Two weeks later he informed me that he'd now told his wife. I didn't have to ask how she'd reacted. His face revealed his relief. Apparently she'd not only responded with love and understanding, she was helping him appraise the extent of their debt and trying to help him get a solution to the whole problem.

She'd even suggested that she try to find a job but both of them had concluded her working at a job wasn't going to be the ultimate answer for them and they'd decided that what they needed was some kind of business of their own, something that interested them both, something they could do together.

They started looking around. They read ads in newspapers and magazines. They consulted business brokers. They considered enterprises as far west as California and as far south as Florida. They nearly bought a general store in Maine.

I wouldn't see him for weeks at a time and then he'd appear again. They had not yet found what they wanted when he told me that he thought he was okay now and really didn't need any more help, that he thanked me very much, I'd been of enormous assistance but he'd like to feel he was on his own. He was sure it was only a matter of time before he and his wife came up with something that was right for them.

"Fine," I said and wished him luck, sure that indeed he and his wife would find what they were looking for eventually, although it wouldn't be a matter of luck but of his changed consciousness.

More than three years passed before I saw him again and then one day he arrived at my office unannounced, waited outside until I was free and then asked if he could speak to me.

"Come on in," I invited, glad to see him. He looked jaunty, trim and happy. I found myself glancing down at his fingernails. They were well-kept and gave no indication of his old habit of biting them down to the quick.

"You look great," I told him.

"I feel great," he answered.

"Things must be going well for you."

"Things are going very well indeed for me. I dropped by to give you this."

He thrust an envelope into my hand. "Open it," he said.

I did and took out a check that was made out to me for $500. "What's this for?" I asked.

"My wife and I kind of figured we owed it to you."

"For what?" I was puzzled. He'd paid me everything he owed me, as far as I could remember.

"Well," he said. "I am proud to inform you that you

142

are now beholding the owner — part owner with my wife — of the Adams Hand-Wrought Jewelry Co. Moreover you are gazing on a man who truly loves his work, who has found his right place, who not only loves his work and is using all his talents and abilities — to quote a number of your favorite phrases — but who is prospering beyond anything he could have envisioned when he met you."

"I'm happy for you, Andrew," I told him, "but there's no need for this." I held out the check.

"No," he said. "Take it. We want you to have it, my wife and I. We'd never have made it without you. And the way we see it, in giving you the $500 check we're just following what you taught me. We're putting money back into circulation, consistent with good." His mouth curved into a grin as he repeated, "Take it. Do you want to start limiting your own prosperity? Besides" — the grin widened — "having put it back into circulation we know it'll return some day, increased and multiplied."

"All right," I answered, "and thank you. As it happens I have a place I'd like to circulate it to." (My nephew's little theatre group needed money for lighting equipment, costumes and scenery.)

"Good," he said. "Then we're both carrying out one of the most important principles of prosperity, aren't we? Putting money back into circulation."

My students have a way of quoting me back to me.

"What kind of jewelry does the Adams Hand-Wrought Jewelry Co. make?" I asked.

Words tumbled enthusiastically from him. "Costume jewelry. But individual, one-of-a-kind pieces. Necklaces, bracelets, armlets, anklets. We even made a tiara, on order from a woman who didn't want to wear her real one to a ball. They're all done by hand. Silver. Some plain. Mostly set with semi-precious stones. Each more beautiful than the one before. My wife and children love them so much they go out to sell them just for the fun of it. The kids take orders after school. Oh, I forgot to tell you. I now sing in a choral group and several of the members belong to firms that are my biggest customers.

"And my wife — she's clever — carries a small case of them around with her wherever she goes and if she's visiting a possible buyer but he says he isn't interested or he's too busy right then, she'll ask if she can leave a brochure with him. Of course he always agrees so she'll open up the case. She always puts the brochures at the very bottom, underneath several rows of the boxed jewelry and she'll take the boxes out one by one and lay them down on a counter, while she's trying to get out the brochure. By the time she finally gets to the bottom of the case the guy has had a good look at various pieces she's brought along — the box covers are transparent — and he nearly always ends up placing an order."

I laughed. "Andrew," I said, "I've never seen your wife but I have a feeling I'd like her very much."

"You would," he assured me. "She's got the right consciousness. And not just in business."

Andrew's last remark reminds me of another wife who was also in business with her husband and who, when they began to lose money badly, came to me for help. As she learned to change her money consciousness she passed the knowledge on to her husband, at times much against his will. But together they finally built the business back up, expanded it and then sold it, realizing a profit ten times their original investment. Later they retired to Spain.

Concha and Juan Limon started out with a mama and papa luncheonette. They made out well enough for awhile and then, for no reason Concha could give me, their business fell off to almost nothing.

Concha had a friend who was in one of my first year Science of Mind classes and she'd been listening to her friend's glowing endorsements of the teaching. One afternoon, worried and desperate, she asked her friend if she could attend a lecture with her. The friend said she'd be delighted.

Concha came and soon she was attending Wednesday evening meetings regularly and eventually she asked me if I'd work with her individually for awhle.

She proved a good student and it wasn't long before she was passing on to Juan all she was learning. Or at least trying to pass it on. I guess Juan wasn't having much of it in the beginning.

"We got to respect and love this business if we want it to prosper," she'd tell him. "That's what this man Eric Pace says. You got to respect and love your work if you want to make it successful. He says poverty is a state of mind and you got to change your state of mind if you want to get out of it. You got to get a prosperity state of mind if you want to prosper."

Although she could see Juan's lack of interest she kept repeating her interpretation of what she was learning and he must have found it penetrating his consciousness for he began to listen, comment or ask questions.

"Juan, he says, this Eric Pace says, you got to love everything in the store and tell it so. Like the grill and the refrigerator and all the stock that comes in. He's not saying they understand. He's saying that's the way to change your consciousness. That's the way to learn to love your business.

"And when a lot of people come in here at a time and it gets kind of hectic we're not supposed to get upset or nervous or wish they wouldn't crowd in all at once because we can't handle them. We're supposed to know we can handle them and the more, the merrier. Because the more that do come in, even all together, the more we're prospering."

"He said that?" Juan shook his head. "That's silly. It's crazy what that man says, Concha. Telling the grill it's great. What kind of nonsense is that? You won't catch me doing that."

"You don't have to do it out loud," Concha would explain earnestly. "And it's not crazy; it works. I believe it works. I'm doing it and we are getting more customers, aren't we?"

They were but Juan wasn't about to grant that it could have anything to do with Concha's changed attitude. Until he noticed that most of the customers seemed to prefer having Concha wait on them to either the counterman or the new waitress they'd had to hire recently. They seemed to like the pleasant way Concha greeted them, the way she joked with them and the careful way she served them.

When he reluctantly spoke about the fact Concha didn't say anything about having told him so. In her way she was as clever as Mrs. Adams. She didn't go rubbing anything in. All she said was, "We got to get them (Max and Bonnie, the counterman and waitress) loving the business too. Loving having more and more customers even though it makes them more work. And I guess the way we do that is to tell them they're going to share in the profits, in our prosperity. The more business we get, the more people pile in here, the more money we'll all be getting together because we'll be giving them raises, we got to tell them. And we got to tell them they should say to themselves, like Eric Pace probably would, 'Boy, it's great, so many people, no chairs empty, no stools, no tables. Because what it means is I'm going to get a raise.'"

"Raise?" Juan wailed. "How we going to give raises? We just beginning to make money. Now you tell me we going to give it out?"

"Sure. That's part of it, Juan. Putting money back into circulation. Because money's a means of exchange and if people aren't exchanging it none of it can come our way."

Juan threw up his hands but he capitulated and the counterman and waitress got their first raises a few months later.

As the business continued to grow, however, people began to complain about having to wait so long for a table.

"We got to expand," Concha told Juan. "We need that extra space next door."

"We can't pay more rent," Juan objected.

"We can. We got to. We got to have the space. If we want the customers. But I been thinking, Juan. We give good service and we give good food. But everything's going up and

146

we haven't ever raised our prices. We're going to have to raise our prices."

"More space! Raise prices! Together?" Juan bawled. "You going to ruin us. I tell you you going to ruin us. We raise prices, we lose customers. What we need extra space for then?"

"We got to be preparing. Looking ahead. I talked about it with Eric Pace. He says if we got to raise prices, then we got to raise them. Maybe, he says, we do lose customers, a few, the first couple days. Some of them may try other places. But if we keep giving good food and good service, he says, they'll come back. Or if they don't we got to know somebody else will take their place.

"Anyhow, Juan, we got to take the chance. Unless you want to be satisfied just making out. I want more. I want we make this luncheonette into a restaurant. Then some day we going to sell the restaurant. Maybe get enough money to go live in Spain like we always talk about."

"My God!" Juan ejaculated. "What you got, Concha, is not a changed consciousness. I tell you. What you got is a crazy consciousness and that's a fact."

But he went along and, as Concha had known it would, her foresight paid off.

For the last six months I've been receiving ecstatic postcards from Spain, signed by Juan and Concha.

CHAPTER XIV

Expanding Your Prosperity

Consciousness

From financial limitation to prosperity — my appointment book abounds with cases of people who have happily made that jump. From inadequate jobs or no jobs at all to successful work in fields the achievers enjoyed — the book has numbers of such feats also. And amazingly these accomplishments have been attained just as frequently during hard times as during times of boom and plenty.

So many. All kinds of people. Young, old. Black, white. Men, women. The educated and those lacking in much formal education. Their age, sex, color, status, didn't matter. All that mattered was that they were each able to change a poverty consciousness to a prosperity consciousness; a limitation consciousness to an expansion consciousness.

I particularly remember Kenny and Jules and Lyle. And there's Fay and Lucy. Oh yes, Charlotte and Alma, too.

Lyle is pushing sixty-two. He's black. He hadn't gone beyond grade-school and he'd always barely made enough money to live on, as a handy-man in a decorator shop that specializes in lamps, from high intensity lights to elaborate chandeliers. With prices rising so rapidly these past few years he could no longer support his wife, himself and his eighty-year-old mother.

When he came to me he was in an acute state of depression but I worked with him to try to discover whether he had talents and abilities he wasn't using and could find a place for or whether he might find a similar job in a larger store where he might have more opportunity for advancement.

I explained to him about enlarging his money consciousness and he listened but he didn't appear to catch on very fast. I gave him a treatment for prosperity and I taught him how to make up treatments of his own and told him to say them over and over again to himself as he went about his daily work.

Weeks passed without any apparent results and then one day he appeared for his appointment, his dark eyes alight with joy.

"Eric," he said as he sat down, "darned if we haven't done it."

"Done what, Lyle?"

"We have changed my consciousness, like you say. Last week a lady came into the shop and she was looking for somebody to clean three chandeliers she has in her apartment. Real elaborate chandeliers. Dozens of crystals. Of course the store don't do work of that kind and couldn't even recommend anyone for her. But I asked the owner if I could have permission to do the job after hours, in my spare time. I told him I really needed the money.

"Well, the owner, he ain't a bad sort and he agreed and the lady was delighted. So I did. I did clean them for her. Day before yesterday and yesterday. I cleaned them chandeliers. And you know what, Eric? I loved that job. I love to see those great, big chandeliers, hanging from the ceilings, clean and glistening. All the pieces of crystal shimmering and shining. It makes my heart feel good just to look at them. And she — the lady — she gave me — well, near a week's salary and she said she was going to tell all her friends about me. All the ones with chandeliers."

"Wonderful, Lyle. Wonderful."

"They're so beautiful, Eric. All those clean, glistening crystals. I could work on them all day and be happy. And the funny thing is I don't need anything except my time — which I got plenty of — and a rag, a ladder and some ammonia and I'm in business for myself."

We both laughed.

But Lyle's subconscious had the last laugh because today he is indeed in business for himself. He quit working at the decorator shop over a year ago and he's working full time at cleaning chandeliers. And he's making a very good living.

Whenever I see him he grins and says, "That old prosperity consciousness, Eric. It's still working. Sometimes it just plain works overtime. If I don't keep it within bounds I'm going to have to hire me an assistant."

Love that man.

Kenny is very different from Lyle. Kenny is white and so young he'd never had a job. And he couldn't seem to get one because he wasn't qualified for anything and had no experience. He also had almost no money and was getting desperate when he came to me.

I talked to him about a money consciousness, about trying to find where his talents and abilities lay, much as I'd talked to Lyle. I also treated for him and taught him to treat on his own and then, just as he was leaving my office something compelled me to say, "Kenny, tell everybody you meet you're looking for work — friends, acquaintances, everybody. Maybe somebody will know of something or see where you'll fit in somewhere that you don't see."

"All right," he agreed listlessly, "but I guess everybody knows. I haven't been keeping it a secret."

"Well, keep on doing it anyway."

Kenny did and finally one of his friends said, "Hey, Kenny, I know a guy. He's a bachelor. Has an apartment. Travels a lot. No time to take care of it. It's a big apartment, with lots of heavy furniture and he can never find anyone to clean it. I told him about you and he says if you want to give it a thorough cleaning — he's fussy — when he says thorough, he means thorough. Move and vacuum behind beds and sofas. Dust pictures, anything high up that most people miss. If you'll really clean it, he'll give you a fair price. He's generous. You and he won't have any trouble agreeing on what it's worth."

As I said, Kenny was almost at the end of his rope. "Sure I'll do it," he answered.

But he wasn't very enthusiastic, he told me. The job didn't seem very manly to him. He shrugged his shoulders. "I'm glad for the money," he admitted, "but it certainly isn't going to lead to much of a career."

He was wrong about that. The bachelor friend of his friend was so pleased with the way his apartment looked when he returned home that he asked Kenny if he'd do the same job for another bachelor he knew.

"I'm still treating for a prosperity consciousness and the right job for me," Kenny told me when next he came to my office. "And it looks like I'm getting the consciousness and the money but whoever heard of a man cleaning apartments for a living?"

"Why not?" I asked. "Lots of people feel guilty about asking women to do certain heavy cleaning for them. Like moving sofas, beds, grand pianos and big, upholstered chairs. You don't dislike doing it, do you?"

He shook his head. "No, I got a lot of energy that's been going to waste and it feels good to use it for a change." And then he fell silent, thinking about what I'd just said. "You know," he finally murmured, "maybe you've got something. Maybe I could turn it into some kind of business. You think there are enough people who need such a service?"

"I think there well may be, if you start treating that there are and that they'll find you or you'll find them."

That was a couple years ago. Once in awhile I see one of Kenny's ads in a newspaper or I tell someone where to find him in the yellow pages of the telephone book.

Kenny's an executive now. He no longer goes out and

does the cleaning himself. He stays home, answers the phone, sends out other young men to do what he once did alone, in teams of two, checks on their work and makes sure it's always thorough.

Kenny suffered from a misconception — that house-cleaning isn't manly. Actually, because men are generally physically stronger, they're often more suited to the type of housework that requires heavy moving than women are.

Charlotte is another student who suffered from a misconception, only in her case there was much apparent truth behind what she believed. She was convinced that she couldn't get pay equal to what she's worth because she's a woman. She was certain that, no matter how good a job she did, she was always going to get a lower wage than the men doing the same work in any company she'd ever work for.

I pointed out to her that she was under an old pattern of belief, a race-mind idea, that women automatically get lower salaries than men for the same work. But she could prove her point; statistics show that women are indeed discriminated against and I had to agree with her.

"But only on the basis of statistics," I told her. "And you're not a statistic. You're an individual. A lot of the women who make up those statistics are where they are because they too haven't been able to shake off the same misconception you have. They feel it's no use to try to fight the discrimination.

"But times are changing. Tell me something. Why do you think the situation occurred in the first place?"

She looked puzzled.

"I mean, why do you think men have generally gotten the higher wages? Because they're just naturally more intelligent?"

She bridled a little but she was no militant feminist. After a moment's hesitation she said softly, "No."

"Then, why?" I pressed.

"Well, I guess it started because at first it wasn't the custom for most women to get educated or work at all, outside of the house. Then when they did begin to get educated and go into business, most of them were married too and their pay checks were just supplementary income for the family.

"Yes, but now? Now many women are just as educated as their male counterparts and many of them are not choosing to marry. So they're the heads of their family, whatever it may consist of. Their incomes aren't supplementary any more. Their incomes are the only ones their families have.

"Now, look, Charlotte, you went to college. You mostly put yourself through. You have an apartment to keep up. You even help support your parents. You've done and are doing what a lot of bachelors I know have done and are doing. Why aren't you entitled to the same amount they make?"

"Well, I think I am but . . . ."

"You are. That's the only answer. And there's no 'but.' Your income should be the result of the work you do. If it isn't, it's because you're not expecting it to be. Why don't you begin quietly to let management know just what you're doing, how much work. And tell them you're interested in getting ahead so you'd be willing to take on even more responsibility, get extra training if you feel you need any.

"And while you're talking to them keep the subconscious thought from popping into your mind that you're a woman so they're not going to listen or be receptive·or be thinking in any terms except of holding you down or taking advantage of you. Keep thinking of yourself as an individual, a working individual whose sex doesn't enter into the matter at hand. Change your consciousness. Change your belief that because you're a woman you're going to encounter prejudice without fail."

Charlotte did what I told her to do and though she still works for the same company, she is now being groomed for the special position of helping the company recruit more qualified women and then training those women to move into various executive posts, both for the benefit of the women and of the firm.

Interestingly, she tells me it's as often the women's consciousness about their worth she has to change as it is the men's.

Meanwhile her salary has doubled and she expects it to keep on rising.

I have another woman student, Fay, who was also always being underpaid. Until we went to work on the problem. But Fay wasn't a victim of sex discrimination. Fay's only enemy was herself. She's an actress and when she first came to me all she'd do would be to sit and complain, "Eric, if someone else had been offered and taken the roles I've had, she'd have been paid more than I've been. Every time. I just know it's true."

"Okay," I eventually pinned her down. "Why aren't you?"

"I don't know." She squirmed.

"Then, think about it. I'd be willing to wager it's because you don't think you're worth any more than you get. Or that the roles you get aren't worth any more than you get paid for playing them."

"Well, I'm a little afraid they mightn't take me if I asked for more money. I admit that. And of course what I mostly get paid is good, in a way, considering the business and the number of people in competition."

"There you are," I said. "You're thinking all wrong in two directions. You're worth what you're convinced you're worth so don't go around resenting someone who thinks she's worth more. Also, because you think the salary you get paid is mostly good, considering the business, that's the level of salary you're going to keep on getting. Until you start changing your consciousness, both about yourself and the business."

"There's another opening coming up," she revealed. "In the same summer theatre where I've worked the last three years. If they call me for a role . . . ."

"If they call you for a role, you will accept the challenge and you will ask them for more money."

"But . . . ."

"You will ask them for more money, knowing that you're

worth it and that the business can well afford to pay it to you."

Actually when the director of the summer theatre called her, as he did, he asked her to play two roles.

She told me about it the following week.

"I said to him — my knees were shaking — I said to him, 'I'd love to do them both. But you know I'm a wife and a mother and I've just got to have . . . .'" (She named a salary much higher than anything they'd paid her in the past).

"And?"

"All he said was, 'Fine, Fay, I understand. I'll mail you the contract this afternoon.'"

(Incidentally, she got rave reviews).

Fay had really only one problem, her evaluation of herself, her self-image, but Lucy, another student of mine, was struggling with several. Recently divorced, she was at loose ends socially. She was living with her mother, whom she largely supported, because she couldn't afford to maintain two households. The arrangement wasn't satisfactory to either of them. They fought constantly. Lucy did have a job she loved — sales manager for business machines — but the pay was so far below her needs that she had to keep hounding her boss for a raise, even though he always reacted angrily whenever she broached the subject.

On her first visit to me we explored a possible change of job, along with a change in consciousness, but she really loved her job and wanted to stay in it.

"Can he—your boss—afford to pay you more?" I asked.

"He says he can't."

"Then we'll just have to treat for supply, from expected and unexpected sources, for money to meet your needs, and let the Law decide where it's coming from."

But the next day she again asked her boss for a raise and this time he exploded and fired her.

She phoned me in panic and we talked awhile on the phone. As we ended the conversation she suddenly said, "You know, in a way, maybe it's a good thing. I'd never have quit myself. Maybe now I'll have the courage to look for something else. Maybe I even belong somewhere else and this was the way I had to find it out."

"Good girl," I approved. "Keep in touch and keep treating for abundance and the right job for you."

(Her boss phoned, by the way, early the next morning, to beg her to come back, said he'd been angry and lost his temper, but she'd made up her mind the firing had been an omen and she refused).

Less than two weeks later she phoned me again. "I have it!" she exclaimed. "The right job for me. The same kind of work. And it just solves all my other problems too. Because the company's in Philadelphia. I'll be getting away from my mother because she wouldn't think of moving to Philadelphia. And I got a big raise so I can afford to keep her here and me there. I'll be in totally new surroundings too. So I just might find some new friends, maybe even a man friend."

Jules, too, like Lucy, had exactly the work that was right for him. He was a designer of custom-made, modern furniture and he was good at it. Still he wasn't doing well financially. His income was definitely below his potential. On occasion he had a hard time making ends meet.

Trying to develop in Jules a prosperity consciousness was almost impossible, so deeply was a failure consciousness embedded in his subconscious. He had a firm belief that nothing good could ever happen to him and that whatever did happen would have to be bad. And naturally he had a long list of failures to prove his contention.

So I decided the best way to deal with Jules was to take a completely different tack.

"When you go out to sell, Jules," I told him, "the best way of licking your problem is to concentrate on the other fellow's prosperity. Plan and figure out how your designs are going to be so successful to the makers that they're going to sell more and more units, thereby becoming more and more prosperous.

"Sure, their prosperity is going to rub off on you but don't let your mind dwell on that. With your self-image you'd sabotage your success. Just keep your mind concentrated on how your new designs will improve your clients' prosperity."

Fortunately, Jules was able to adopt such an approach with moderate assurance and gradually his sales began to increase, as did his own prosperity. But it was nearly a year— a year of consistent treatment work—before Jules could change from thinking of his clients' prosperity to his own and to believing that good is as available to him as it is to anybody else. If you have trouble changing your consciousness, try this method. It works because any solution to any problem you have involves the good of all concerned, not only yourself.

Irrational thinking takes so many devious forms that stratagems like the one that worked for Jules have to be used to counteract it. This is especially true when we're trying to replace limitation by abundance.

When you begin to give yourself a treatment for anything, not only limitation, you should keep in mind that, though within the Infinite Intelligence the possibilities of creation are limitless, within you they tend to be limited, at least for the moment, by where you are in consciousness at the particular time you start treating.

In other words, if you have a $100 a week consciousness to begin with, it is unlikely that you are going to be able to change it overnight into a $1,000 a week consciousness.

You have to start from where you are. If you don't have some understanding of this fact you may reach too far and too fast and let yourself in for disappointment and disillusionment. You may even give up using Science of Mind and thereby lose a technique that I believe is invaluable for improving the quality of anyone's life.

The thing to do is to recognize where you are in consciousness, set realistic goals for yourself, consistent with the level of that consciousness, and expand them as you expand your consciousness.

Recently a young girl came to see me. She's a typist and she's making $88 a week but she'd heard about Science of

Mind and had decided she wanted me to help her get a salary of $200 a week.

"It's a reasonable goal," I told her, "but I hope you're not expecting to reach it by next week."

She frowned uncertainly so I tried to explain. "Can you imagine yourself collecting a pay check of $200 by next week and for your work as a typist?"

She pushed her tongue against her upper lip and concentrated. I could see she was having to struggle. "Why not think first in terms of a raise from $88 to $100 a week?" I suggested. "Work toward your goal in steps. Enlarge your horizon by taking a course to become a secretary. You can visualize getting a pay check of $100, can't you, if not by next week at least very shortly?"

Her whole face brightened as she nodded.

"Good," I said. "Then we'll begin with $100 and keep expanding."

I'll repeat, for emphasis, because the point is so important. Starting from the place where she was in financial consciousness she had to start at a level of about $100 a week because a weekly paycheck of $100 was about all she could manage to conceive of herself as having for the present.

But I have another student who phones me frequently to request a treatment for money. He's an art dealer and $50,000 is the least he ever wants me to treat for. His level of consciousness is never far below $50,000 and can expand to twice that amount when necessary.

When I started raising my own level of money consciousness I set no particular goal for myself beyond acquiring whatever amounts I might need for more ease and more comfort and more freedom of choice. My prosperity consciousness had never been too high and certainly not consistently so and I knew I held a number of negative beliefs about money.

I began by concentrating on learning to love and respect the bills in my wallet, to treat them with as much care as I'd give to those things I did love and respect and find beautiful, like flowers. Even if I acquired a bill of only one dollar I would unfold it carefully, smooth its wrinkled edges and place it gently in my wallet with the other bills there, which I was now arranging in ascending order, smaller denominations in the back, larger ones in a progression toward the front and all neatly facing the same way.

And whatever the denomination, small or large, I would take a moment mentally to approve of it, welcome it and visualize an even larger denomination replacing it as it circulated to fulfill its purpose. Today I still find myself following much the same procedure, though less consciously, of course.

I taught myself also to rejoice in every event in which an immediate, subconscious action of mine revealed to me an expanding prosperity consciousness.

My final story involving a changed money consciousness concerns Alma, one of the first students at the New Jersey Center, and I'm going to give it to you in her own words as she told it one day at a Friday noon meeting which was being recorded on tape by another student.

We'd been discussing prosperity and somebody remarked he'd heard about a marvelous demonstration Alma had made in that area and would Alma tell about it?

Alma glanced at me. I'm always cautioning people against taking over a meeting or lecture and giving any kind of testimonial that takes time and prevents others from asking questions and participating. But everybody seemed to be talked out and a number of heads were turned toward Alma, their owners looking interested, so I nodded at her to go ahead.

"Well, it's kind of fantastic. It really is. I wouldn't have believed it could happen the way it did."

On the tape Alma's voice bubbles as it did in the lecture hall:

"When Eric first talked about going out to the seminar in San Francisco last spring I knew I wanted to go. Real bad. But I couldn't figure out how I could possibly get enough money. I went home and looked at my bank book and I had maybe $90. Ninety when what I needed was close to $400.

"My goodness, I thought, why do I get ridiculous notions like thinking I can go to San Francisco for a week, to a seminar, when all I have is $90.

"Still I wanted to go. Real bad, as I said, and that night I couldn't stop thinking about it. I was so preoccupied that Herman, my husband, finally asked me what was wrong. I told him about the seminar and how much I wished I could go although I knew it was impossible.

" 'How much do you have in your account?' he asked me.

" 'Ninety dollars,' I said.

" 'Well, I tell you what,' he told me. 'I can't give you the money. I don't have it right now but I'll borrow it. I'd like you to go too. So you can be with your friends.'

"I thought about it and then I shook my head. 'No,' I told him, 'I don't think that's the way a treatment for money would work. I've been treating but well . . . . No, I don't think that would really be a demonstration. Our having to borrow money. I don't want us to have to borrow money, especially now when things are going kind of nice for us and we have no big bills.'

" 'Well,' Herman said, 'keep it in mind anyway. Okay?'

"I agreed but I felt sure there had to be another way so I made up my mind to talk to Eric about it. 'Look,' I told Eric, 'I really want to go to this seminar but I don't have the money and I don't know how I can get it.'

"And Eric's answer was, 'You really want to go? If you do you'll just tell yourself you know you're going, stop futzing around and treat for the means to get there—money from expected and unexpected sources. Know it's available and you've just got to accept it in your experience.'

"Well, I guess that was some time in February and in March, for some unknown reason . . . . You all know I'm an artist? I mean I teach but I paint too. I sort of specialize in these what I call 'frescoes.' Paintings in a kind of sculpture relief. Well, in March, for some unknown reason, I began to get calls for them. From galleries where I'd exhibited them a couple or more years ago and they'd been rejected. I mean they hadn't sold. The galleries had gotten so sick of having them around they'd asked me to take them back and I'd put them in the attic and actually forgot I had some of them.

"But now I began to get these phone calls from the galleries and I said to them, 'Well, you know, I haven't got time to make new stuff right now. I'm very busy. So all I can do is bring out some of my old stuff that everybody's seen and nobody wanted.'

"'That's all right,' they answered. 'We're getting calls for them.'

"Getting calls for them two or more years after people have seen them and didn't want them, I thought to myself. That's funny. It doesn't make sense. But who am I to question a sale? If they wanted them I'd bring them over.

"So I brought a bunch of them to the three galleries that had phoned me and I made about $300 in like about a week. People—they just bought them. It was unbelievable. I tried to find out from the galleries what had happened but all they could tell me was that people had begun to wander in and say they remembered being there a couple years ago and seeing some work by an Alma Tesch and they'd decided they'd like to buy one of the frescoes and hang it in their grouping.

"I mean the galleries were just as stunned as I was, after having to ask me to remove all the stuff because they'd had it so long without any action. They hadn't been able to afford to have it taking up wall space.

"And one night I said to my husband, 'It's so odd, all this that's been happening, me selling all these things nobody wanted before. I'm having to go up in the attic and look through my junk-junk.

"'What's so odd about it?' Herman said. 'If you're treating every day for the money to go to the seminar, what's so odd about getting a demonstration for your treatments?'

"'Why, of course. That's right,' I said. I was surprised I hadn't thought of that myself.

"Then I told Eric what was happening. I told him, 'I'm selling all kinds of stuff. All the work I couldn't move nohow.

Would you believe it? Three hundred dollars in like about a week.'

" 'Alma,' Eric said to me, 'Demonstrations are supposed to follow treatments.'

" 'That's what Herman said,' I answered. 'You'd think I'd know that by now.' "

Alma told her story at a meeting in which we'd all been discussing ways and means of improving our prosperity consciousness. I ended that meeting as I always do by giving a combination meditation and short treatment. The meditations and treatments I give at the end of such meetings usually center around whatever we've been discussing; so that day they centered around prosperity.

Since I think you might like to use them to apply in changing your own prosperity consciousness I am including them here, as transcribed from the tape of the student who also recorded Alma's story.

Although it is my custom to give meditations and treatments at meetings or lectures in the first person plural this time when I come to the part that is strictly treatment I shall give it in the first person singular; so that as you read it, it becomes personal to you. It becomes your own individual treatment which you can read over and over to yourself, to impress into your consciousness.

The meditation and treatment follow:

We have talked today about the idea of being surrounded by a Creative Intelligence. We have affirmed that we are that Creative or Infinite Intelligence individualized and that we therefore have the right to direct our thinking. More than that—we have the responsibility of directing our thinking. Because we know that this Infinite Mind responds to us by corresponding.

We have talked about thinking only upon those things which we desire to experience and that the Absolute Mind corresponds by reproducing in our outer world our inner thought patterns. Mostly we have talked about having a good prosperity consciousness.

So now let's do what we've talked about so long. Let's neutralize the things in our consciousness we no longer want there and let's think upon those things that we do want.

We begin by visualizing ourselves totally surrounded by a great Energy, a Creative Force, Mind, Intelligence, however you want to think·of It. And then we tell ourselves and know that this Force, Energy, Mind, Intelligence, Power, which surrounds us takes the impress of our thought and produces out of Its own substance our thought into a thing, a form, a condition, an experience. It does this because that is the way It works, that is the law of Its being. And since we are one with this Power, Force, Life, Love, Energy, Mind, Intelligence, this Totality, there is no reason for us to know lack or limitation. There is no place where this Intelligence ends and we begin and no place where we end and this Intelligence begins. Therefore good, our good, is always at hand wherever we are. All we desire is available to us and we now place ourselves in perfect order; so that our thought processes bring about the experiences we want in our lives.

"There is one Cause, one Power, One Intelligence, in all, through all, as all; therefore It is in me right where I am.

"So I now set myself free from any disorderly ideas I have ever had about the world of form and finance. I refuse to be disorderly about money, food, clothing, transportation, shelter or other things of such nature. I no longer believe in lack or limitation. I no longer believe in any negative concepts about money. I no longer·believe that poverty is a virtue, that the love of money is the root of all evil, that I am not worthy of prosperity, or that I have to rob another to obtain it or that another has to rob me for him to obtain it.

"I don't care how long I have had these negative beliefs and patterns in my subconscious mind, nor where I got them, who taught them to me or why I continue to hold them. I now neutralize them. I now de-emotionalize them in my subconscious as well as my conscious mind.

"I have orderly patterns of prosperity because I love the line, bulk, texture and design of the Universe. I love them when they are called a rose. I love them when they are called food or shelter. I love them when they are called money, the shape and form which is used to exchange ideas, goods and services. I am comfortable with every form the Absolute Mind creates and I always have those forms which create ease, pleasure and beauty. I am open and receptive to prosperity in my life. Right here and right now. And so it is."

CHAPTER XV

How to Attract

Loving Relationships

It's love, says an anonymous poet, it's love that makes the world go round.

If there is one thing that the field of science has learned it is that absolute statements are dangerous. The truth of today is almost certain to be questioned and proved partial and inadequate or totally false tomorrow. The same can be said of the field of human relationships and affairs.

And yet, through the ages, one quality does seem to stand out clearly as the quality above all others without which our world and even the cosmos itself would eventually cease to exist. And that quality is love.

What is evolution, the first and basic law of the universe, but the love of the Infinite Intelligence expressing Itself through the creation of ever new, higher, more complicated, more adaptable forms, always with a greater tendency toward perfection?

On the cosmic scale, then, Infinite Love appears as the ceaseless action of creation, in which that which is created is ever more developed, ever more evolved, ever more an expression reaching toward perfection.

On the human scale, love can perhaps best be defined as a sense of knowing that you are one with this Infinite Love; that you are Its creation at a point of individualization; that you are part of Its action; that you are the outlet for Its expression in the world of your experience; that you are love and cannot be otherwise because It is Love and you are one with It.

And the way that you express love is by recognizing that what you are, every other person, place and thing also is.

Whether we are talking about universal or human love, we are, in a sense, then, talking about the same thing. The quality of love is not different in its unity or oneness; it is different only in its expression and in the object on which it bestows its expression.

Some people who find themselves failing to communicate with fellow humans run to communicate with the Infinite. Others, with the opposite problem do the opposite thing. Both courses are dodges. Both are ways of escaping from hurts, disappointments, misunderstandings. Behind both is a desire to repudiate, reject, deny.

Both are doomed to foster feelings of separation, isolation, desperation and desolation.

If love is sensing the unity, the oneness of all in the One, then you either have to encompass all in your love or you are encompassing none.

Now I don't mean you have to love every person, place and thing in such a way as to want them in your world, intimately or indeed at all. You love because they are manifestations of the Infinite Love but you may not like how they are behaving, what they are thinking or how they are choosing to manifest.

No, you don't have to like and condone something or someone you don't approve of or believe in. At least I don't and can't. I draw a distinction between loving what a person is (the Infinite Love personified) and what that person, by his or her free will, is doing (how that Infinite Love is being expressed through human choice).

I can dislike a person. I can be annoyed or disturbed by someone or his attitude or the way he views life. I can even not want him to touch my experience and yet I don't have to reject him. I don't have to show hate. I can be angry with a person for something he's done because I think it's not right or it's hurt my feelings and still not lose the basic idea of love, the sense that what I am, he too is.

Some of my students get very caught up in the idea that they have to love everyone in the sense of embracing everyone in their world and I guess that's fine if you can do it and I guess that makes them more evolved than I am. Because I can't. There are some people I don't like. Some people I don't want in my world, in my experience.

For, as I said, I make a distinction. I may dislike, may not approve of, may get angry at, may be annoyed by someone's action but I try never to disapprove of the person himself. For I know I'd then be disapproving of Love Itself.

To me, the first attitude is a human reaction, natural on this human plane of action. The second is a deeply unloving state of mind that is the cause of most of our own and the world's problems.

One day after a noon lecture I was having lunch with a group of friends when I noticed a middle-aged woman, sitting alone at a booth across from us. I had a feeling that I had been drawn to look at her because she had been staring at me but as soon as she saw me glance toward her she dropped her eyes to her plate and closed in on herself with little hunching movements of her head and shoulders.

Do I know her? I asked myself. She seemed familiar and yet I couldn't place her. Moreover she acted and was dressed so strangely that if I had known her I surely ought to have remembered where and when. She stood out in the restaurant just off fashionable Fifth Avenue where we were all eating. It was late fall and she wore a cotton house dress, a sacklike long-sleeved sweater, white ankle socks and white sneakers. Her hair could have been beautiful for it was thick and wavy but it was pulled back from her face, held together by an elastic band and knotted in a round, tight ball at the back of her head. On the floor, on both sides of her feet, were string shopping bags, bulging with packages and papers.

Still puzzled by the vague feeling of knowing her and yet not knowing her, I was about to ask if anyone at the table had an idea of who she was but at the moment everyone was busy talking so rather than interrupt I let the matter go.

But when we were all leaving she again looked up from her plate and this time shot a side-long, tentative glance at Karen and an apologetic, half-smile touched her lips.

Outside I said to Karen, "Who was that?"

"Who was who?" Karen asked.

"Who was that woman back there who smiled at you?"

"Don't you know?"

"Would I have asked if I did?"

"Well, I don't know her name," Karen answered. "But I thought you might. That's what I meant when I asked if you didn't know. Don't you remember her? She lives in your neighborhood. You must have seen her any number of times shopping at Peter Reeves."

And suddenly I did remember. She was the woman who, whenever she reached the cash register, always seemed to hold up the line forever while she counted out the money for her purchases in pennies, nickles, dimes and quarters.

"Besides," Karen added, "she's been auditing your classes for at least three years and has never missed one that I know of."

Auditing my classes for three years and I'd still managed to miss seeing her, the way she looked! "Poor thing," I found myself murmuring.

"I take it you don't mean because she's been listening to you lecture for three years," Karen teased.

"Do you know anything more about her?" I asked.

Karen shook her head. And then, "Oh, yes. I did hear

that she comes from some small town in Texas and that rather than being the poor thing you think she is, she's rich. Her father struck oil or something, died and left her all his money."

"She may be rich in money," I said, "but she's poorer in love—self-love at any rate—than anyone I've seen in a long time. Moreover, unless I miss my guess, she's lonely. Very lonely. It's funny how lonely, odd people always manage to gravitate toward a big city so they can get lost in the crowd and be even more lonely."

"That doesn't sound logical," Karen objected. "I'll bet they come because they think that, among all the people here, somebody will be friends with them."

"Consciously, yes," I agreed. "But actually they're following the old rejection pattern that made them lonely and odd in the first place."

"Well . . . ." Karen was not convinced. "She does keep to herself in class but she smiles at people. Like she smiled back there. I know it's the kind of smile that makes you think she expects you to hit her and of course I never see her talking to anyone but I thought that was because nobody ever talks to her. What could one talk to her about? I guess we all feel there'd be no use in trying. She's so obviously not with it. But if she's really lonely as you say she is—if she wants friends—then why doesn't she act friendly?"

"Because she doesn't know how. She doesn't know that if she wants friends, if she wants love, she's going to have to learn to love. And she's going to have to start by learning to love herself. Until she realizes that she herself is Love, she's never going to realize that anybody else is either. So she's never going to call it out in anybody." I broke stride and mused to myself, "Three years and I haven't gotten that across to her. I wonder why?"

Karen too slowed and then she put her hand on my arm. "If she listens, Eric, and doesn't hear, what can you do about it? But I'll tell you what. I'll talk to her next time

I see her in class. I'll try being friendly. Maybe she'll respond."

"Good girl," I said because I didn't want to discourage her but I doubted she'd have much success.

We soon fell to discussing other things and I must confess I forgot all about the middle-aged waif back in the restaurant until months later when she appeared at my office for an appointment my secretary had made for her. I looked down at my appointment book and matched the 3 o'clock entry there with the apparently perennial cotton dress, sweater, ankle socks and sneakers. "Miss Wiley?"

"Yes. Sheila Wiley."

I had forgotten her but as I later learned, Karen hadn't. She did talk to Sheila Wiley the next time they met and continued to talk to her until one day Sheila had hesitantly told her that she appreciated Karen's trying to be friends but she really didn't want to put her out any more. "It's kind of you and I am grateful," Sheila had whispered doggedly, "but I'm just not very good at what Mr. Pace calls relationships. I never have been. Not even back home in Texas when I was little. I always thought maybe it was because I wasn't pretty but maybe I wouldn't have been anyway."

Karen had never been a girl to miss an opportunity and she didn't miss this one. What she said or how she persuaded Sheila she's never made quite clear to me but there was Sheila telling me that she wanted to work with me personally.

"About forming better relationships," Sheila said into the hand that was cupped around her mouth.

"You've been coming to my classes for sometime, isn't that true?"

Sheila bobbed her head.

"Then I'm sure you've heard me say before that in order to be able to love, in order to be able to form loving relationships, you first have to love yourself."

Again the head bobbed and from behind the cupped hand Sheila said, "Yes. But that's the trouble. I can't. I just can't love myself."

"You can't love yourself because you're thinking of yourself as somebody not worthy of being loved. You are not
thinking of yourself as somebody through whom, in whom
and as whom the Infinite Love is expressing Itself."

Sheila dropped her hand and a spark of something close
to anger appeared in her eyes. "Oh, I try," she assured me,
"but then something inside me says, 'Well, if that's what It's
doing, It isn't doing a very good job.' Because look at me, Mr.
Pace. Just look at me."

So she had some awareness of her oddness, I realized.
That was a plus. "It isn't doing any kind of a job, Miss Wiley,"
I answered, "and never can except the kind of job you force
It to do through the state of your own consciousness. By your
own opinions of yourself, the feelings and thoughts you hold
of yourself, you are literally forcing It to do what you call not
a very good job. You know that. You must. You must have
heard me say something of the sort innumerable times."

"Yes," she admitted. "Only for me it's the old vicious
circle. I can't love myself so I can't project love so I can't attract love. So when I can't attract love then I can't love myself
and then I can't project . . . . See what I mean? Oh, I don't
know why I came. It's hopeless."

If that was as far as her consciousness could expand at
the moment then she was indeed in a vicious circle. Racking
my brain for a way to help her break out of it, I suddenly
thought of a story a young girl had once told me. I like to use
stories to illustrate a point. I find most people not only get the
point faster but with less effort and more enjoyment.

"Miss Wiley," I said, "I don't know whether you know
. . . . You probably do. You've probably heard me refer at least
once at one of my lectures to when I was in the theatre. At
the particular time I want to tell you about I was directing a
play. In summer stock. In Massachusetts. There was a young
girl playing the ingenue role and the newspapers invariably
described her as beautiful. I suppose those of us who worked
with her would also have described her the same way, if we'd
been asked. She walked with her head held high, in long

graceful strides. She looked healthy. Her skin glowed. Her eyes sparkled. Her hair gleamed. She had a face that gave the impression of having been chiseled. But the thing you noticed most about her was that she seemed to feel beautiful.

"Yes, I can't remember anybody who saw her who didn't remark on her beauty.

"And then one day her sister came to see the play and she visited backstage afterward. And now we were confronted with two girls who closely resembled each other except that one was truly beautiful. Classically beautiful. Perfect features. Perfect nose. Perfect mouth. Perfect teeth. Perfect body. And that one wasn't our young ingenue, Regina. It was her sister, Vivian.

"For awhile cast and crew all found the situation surprising, even upsetting. We began to look at Regina in a different light. Because the resemblance between the sisters was so strong we began to make comparisons. Regina's nose wasn't so perfect, her teeth weren't so perfect, her mouth wasn't so perfect, even her body wasn't so perfect as her sister's.

"If Regina noticed the change in our attitudes she gave no sign. She went right on walking with her head high, her back straight, looking healthy, at peace and with that air of feeling beautiful.

"And gradually, Miss Wiley, we lost our confusion and returned to our original conception of her, the one she obviously held of herself—that whether hers was a conventional beauty or not it was beauty. As great as her sister's. Different but as great.

"A few of us even came to the conclusion that it was greater than her sister's. I was one of them.

"Vivian and Regina were, it was easy to see, on good terms and fond of each other. They talked about family matters, laughed a lot and seemed proud of each other. Vivian was married and had two children about whom Regina couldn't hear enough. She kept exclaiming over photographs and anecdotes about them. Vivian, on her part, was fascinated with Regina's work in the theatre and made no secret of her pride in Regina's success. Only once did I notice the faintest shadow fall across this picture of affection and that was when Vivian, who had been calling her sister, Gina, suddenly called her Duck instead.

"For a moment Regina seemed to freeze. The sparkle left her eyes and she turned her head away.

I had been standing nearby, neither listening nor trying to avoid listening. As I said the conversation was mostly about family, idle and of no importance that I could tell. But now, for no apparent reason, I felt as if I'd been eavesdropping and I hastened to move away but before I could get out of earshot I heard Vivian apologize, 'Sorry, Gina. Really. I didn't mean it. It just slipped out. Forgive me.'

"Regina laughed and answered, 'Sure. Nothing to forgive, Viv. We were talking about old times and I guess it's natural to connect old names with old times.'

"I was curious, in spite of myself, Miss Wiley, and I thought, Old names? What could Regina have meant? Had Duck once been her nickname? If so, she didn't seem to like it and I didn't blame her. I didn't like it either. To me it had a low-class English ring to it and was singularly inappropriate for our regal Regina.

"I didn't realize until after Vivian had gone that Regina had seen my hasty retreat and knew I had heard the slight dissonance that had occurred between the two sisters.

"Most of the cast and crew were gone for the day and I was sitting down in one of the front orchestra seats going over in my mind possible improvements in one of the scenes that wasn't playing well when Regina appeared and sat in the seat next to me.

" 'Very busy, Mr. Pace?' she asked.

" 'Not too, Regina,' I told her.

" 'I know you heard back there, didn't you? I don't mean you were listening but I know you couldn't help hearing that little argument—no, not argument—that little display of touchiness I showed when Vivian called me Duck.'

" 'Yes,' I admitted, 'though not, as you say, because I was actually listening. But we all get touchy now and then. Don't worry about it.'

" 'I'm not worried about it,' Regina asserted. 'But because you did hear I thought you might like to know what it's all about. I've heard you're a believer in Science of Mind, Mr. Pace. That you study and practice it.'"

I broke off my story to explain to Miss Wiley, "The last few years before I left the theatre to teach Science of Mind I'd been a student at the old headquarters and of course I'd been practicing it."

Miss Wiley gave the now familiar little bob of her head.

"I told Regina that I did indeed believe in and practice Science of Mind," I went on.

" 'Then,' she said, 'I'm sure you'll be interested in how I got the nickname Duck. Actually the full nickname should have been Ugly Duckling but it got shortened to Duck by Viv because when she first heard it she was too small to say the whole thing. You see when I was a child I wasn't very good-looking. To be honest, I guess I was ugly. At least that's what my Aunt Charlene thought.

" 'And that, Mr. Pace, was more of a tragedy in my family,' Regina continued, 'than it might have been in some other. Because the whole family, on both sides, had always been— oh, great beauties, in the case of the women. Handsome bucks, in the case of the men. And here was I, an outstanding exception. And to make it worse, Vivian, who's four years younger, was following the family pattern spectacularly.

" 'Well, as no doubt you're aware, Mr. Pace, people can be cruel. Or thoughtless, if you prefer a euphemism. Someone was always commenting on what a pity it was that we were so different, Viv and I, she so beautiful and I so plain. But it was my tactless, imperious Aunt Charlene who capped my misery and gave me the nickname people picked up from Viv. One day when I was eight Aunt Charlene remarked something to the effect that she didn't know who I took after. Not, she said, the Stedmans. Aunt Charlene's my father's sister.

No, she was sure I didn't take after the Stedmans. And then she conceded that I didn't take after the Cornwalls either. My mother's a Cornwall. Finally she decided that I must be a throw-back to some remote ancestor she'd never heard of and concluded her flattering discourse by lamenting that if I had to be an ugly duckling it was too bad I hadn't been born a boy.

" 'I like to think that Aunt Charlene didn't realize that I was old enough to understand. But I suspect that comes under the heading of wishful thinking. Anyway it doesn't matter. She really did me a big favor. Viv did too, in a way. At four the words ugly duckling meant nothing to her. Moreover she couldn't even get her tongue around them. When she tried she had to settle for calling me a mere duck. She knew that word because we had one. But I suppose it was really my fault that the nickname stuck. Because if I hadn't been so humiliated and yelled at Viv she might have forgotten the whole business.

" 'But I did yell and Vic has a stubborn streak when it's aroused. My yelling at her aroused it. So she called me Duck again. I yelled again.

" 'That's the way it started,' Regina said. 'I don't remember how other people came to pick it up until it became a nickname but they did and I had to learn to live with it. Until Viv was thirteen. By then we were friends as well as sisters so one day I pleaded with her please to call me Gina from then on because I hated being called Duck.

" 'That's when I found out she had no recollection of how the nickname had originated or who had originated it. When I told her she was contrite and promised that she'd never call me Duck again and that she'd make everyone else stop also. But she was angry too. Angry at Aunt Charlene. She thought it was mean of Aunt Charlene to have talked the way she had. Around us. So I could hear. She said she thought Aunt Charlene must have been crazy and blind too because I was beautiful. Everybody thought I was beautiful. Surely I must be aware of that.

" 'And do you know, Mr. Pace,' Regina told me simply, 'what she said was true. By then most people had begun to think of me as beautiful. I'm not being conceited. I'm just stating a fact. Because what I really want to tell you, what I know you'll be interested in, is that I hadn't just outgrown my ugliness, as perhaps you may be thinking. I'd programed myself out of it.

" 'How it happened was, on the day that my Aunt Charlene called me an ugly duckling, I made up my mind that I was going to be beautiful. Some day. Somehow. Later, that afternoon, I went to my room, sat down at my dressing table and looked at myself in the mirror. What I saw there wasn't too far off from Aunt Charlene's description and I don't know how I was lucky enough to hit on the practice I did. Maybe I have more than a little of Viv's stubborness.

" 'Anyway I looked at that mirrored image of me and I said aloud to it and myself, It's a lie. I'm not ugly. I'm beautiful. My face is beautiful. My eyes are beautiful. My skin is beautiful. My hair is beautiful. My nose is beautiful. My teeth are beautiful. My body is beautiful. It's healthy and I walk straight and with my head up. Every part of me is beautiful, from the top of my head to the tip of my toes. What's more, I feel beautiful.'

"At this point Regina shifted in her chair, turned full-face to me and said earnestly, 'I was eight years old, Mr. Pace, and I didn't know anything about psychology, the subconscious, how to program it or anything like that. I'm not sure I even knew anything much about having a mind. Certainly I'd never heard of Science of Mind. But I'd hit on a method of what I guess you'd call changing my consciousness. And I never stopped using it. Day after day, week after week, year after year, I told that me in the mirror that it was beautiful. Eventually it seemed to get convinced. And apparently others got convinced also.' "

There was more to Regina's tale but I had told all of it that was necessary and I now endeavored to show Miss Wiley how she could use it to her own benefit. "Why don't you," I suggested to her, "try something like Regina did. Say your treatments every day, of course. But because the negative impression you have of yourself is so strong in your consciousness, because you find it so impossible to conceive of yourself as someone to love, I think, in your case, we might add the procedure of talking to yourself in the mirror, to help buttress your treatments. It's a device that didn't originate with Regina. As she said, she just happened on it. People have been using it a long time.

"Put aside maybe fifteen minutes each day, Miss Wiley, for sitting in front of your mirror, just as Regina did. Look deep into your eyes and say aloud to yourself, 'The Infinite is Love and I am the Infinite expressing Itself through me. Therefore I am love. I am love and first and foremost I love myself. I respect myself. I know myself to be a person of worth. I love myself because I know that until I learn to love the Infinite in me, I can't learn to love the Infinite in anyone else. And because I love myself, I project love and I attract love. So I'm surrounded by love. I'm supported by love. I'm immersed in love. And I refuse to entertain any doubts of the truth of my words. I refuse to listen to any voice within me that would argue otherwise. There is nothing but love and that love objectifies as people, places, and things in my world so that I am no longer lonely. I have all the friends I need and want.'

"Will you try this procedure for at least a couple of weeks, Miss Wiley? I believe you might begin to see a change in that self-destructive consciousness of yours."

Sheila Wiley's lack of love for herself had been too long a part of her for her to have much faith that she could change but she gave an obedient little bob of her head.

I made one further attempt to straighten out her thinking before giving her a treatment. "Try, Miss Wiley," I said, "when you leave here and from now on to keep in mind that when I talk about loving yourself I'm not talking about egotism. I'm not talking about engaging in any search for superiority, any comparisons, adverse or favorable, of yourself with

anyone else. I'm talking about recognition that you are one
with the Infinite Love and that therefore within you is the
same capacity for being, expressing and receiving love as
there is in any other individual anywhere."

Today I count Sheila Wiley as one of the most remarkable demonstrations I've ever come across of how an inner
change in thought patterns can result in an outer change of
experience. Gone are the cotton dresses, the stretched sweat-
ers, ankle socks and sneakers. Gone are the string bags loaded
with the odds and ends she once cherished. Gone is the tight
ball of hair at the back of her neck. Gone is the apologetic
manner, the self-deprecating behavior, the servile bob of the
head.

Today Sheila looks like what she is, a smartly-dressed,
attractive middle-aged woman, loving and loved, a busy, tal-
ented, social-minded woman who divides her time between
the teen-aged children she acquired through marriage to the
doctor who heads the free dental-medical clinic she set up in
one of the poorer areas, her husband and their friends.

And there's a last, amusing note to Sheila's case I'd like
to add here—long after she'd stopped coming to me for personal instruction she smilingly confessed when we were chatting after an evening lecture that she hadn't confined either
treatments or her work in front of the mirror to being able to
love and attract love. Every word she could remember that
I'd told her Regina had said to her mirrored image she too had
said to her own image. "I guess," she admitted, "that what
you told me about Regina made as much impression on me as
anything else you said that first day. You see, I've always
longed to be beautiful, even when, like Regina, I was an ugly
duckling. Oh, I know I'll never make it the way she did. After
all"—she laughed—"she had a good thirty years' start on me.
But at least I don't think many people consider me ugly any
more. Anyway I don't myself."

No. Sheila Wiley Craig's not beautiful in the usual meaning of the word but, for someone her age, she's one of the
most striking women I know.

CHAPTER XVI

Love and You Get
Love Back

We are never out of the action of Love although by our own free will, our negative thoughts and emotions, we can create conditions that bring about its non-appearance, restriction or loss in our experience.

Many people who are lonely and want to demonstrate love and good relationships in their life may not, like Sheila, be lacking totally in self-love. It is, however, my belief that lack of self-love is the primary basis for most feelings of separation and isolation. But some thought patterns that manifest as unloving and unloved relationships stem from a basic misunderstanding of what love is.

Not only is love a cohesive force that brings together those who or that which belong together and separates those who or that which do not belong together, it is the ability or willingness to accept others as the Infinite at a point of specialization. It is the ability and willingness to allow others to be what they wish to be, to demonstrate that specialization as they choose, without the need to dictate, to dominate, to manipulate or to hold on to that which no longer belongs or wants to belong to us.

In my counseling work I am constantly confronted with such mistaken attitudes masquerading as a conviction of love. Every month or two I meet up with a parent who wants to dictate to his or her child what work or profession it shall take up, how it should act, where it should go or not go. But dictating has never been loving and succeeds only in interfering with the creative, dynamic energy within the child that is the Infinite Intelligence expressing Itself in, as and through the child. If parents would try to see the child for what it is— this Creative Force individualized—they would, I believe, be less inclined to oppose and meddle and more able to trust and let be.

Often too I meet up with the wife or husband who uses the tie of love as an excuse for dominating, for bending the other to his or her will, like the husband who came to me recently to ask me to treat that his wife be "more loving and more responsive to my needs." With questioning I discovered that what he meant by wanting her to be more loving and responsive to his needs was that he wanted to be allowed the right to do as he chose in the marriage, without having to consider his wife's rights, feelings or needs. He had a habit of going bowling or card playing after work and not appearing home for dinner and also not bothering to phone his wife that he wasn't going to be home. He also had a habit of promising to take her somewhere or of promising to go somewhere with her and then always finding some justification for being unable to do whatever he'd promised, such as there being a TV program he wanted to see that night, its being too far to drive, too hot or too cold an evening or his just not feeling in the mood.

And what he couldn't understand, he told me, was why his wife wanted to "fence him in" the way she did, why she was unhappy and critical of his behavior. "If she really loved me," he said, "she wouldn't make things so difficult for me. Her demands and objections are making me ill," he complained. "I've told her that. I've told her she's making me ill and she must stop."

I had to explain to him that, first of all, I never give a treatment for someone other than the person asking for it, that I had no right to treat that his wife be any particular way, responsive or otherwise, that such a course would be an attempt to manipulate, to interfere with the right of another—and without that person's consent—to express his or her individuality as he or she sees fit.

"I can only," I told him, "treat for you, for the situation itself and for your response to the situation. Which may, it is true, affect the way your wife responds or acts. But I cannot, in any way, try through treatment to influence the behavior of a third person, a person who has not requested me to treat for him or her."

He couldn't seem to comprehend the difference and because I had no intention of treating his wife—in absentia—to change, he appeared somewhat disillusioned with the whole business.

"I wonder," I finally said to him, "if what you are doing isn't using the love which you say your wife has for you as a weapon to dominate her. How often does she make dinner, sit and watch it grow cold when you haven't even phoned you're not going to be home? How often has she found you unresponsive to her need to attend a party you've promised to take her to? A marriage isn't a relationship in which one partner makes all the decisions or always dominates while the other always has to acquiesce or comply.

"As for her making you ill—no, she's not making you ill. You're making yourself ill. No one can make someone else ill because what makes a person ill is his or her own thought patterns, not those of someone else. Your health or lack of it is a result of your consciousness about what your physical body is, a manifestation of what the Infinite Intelligence meant it to be—perfect—or a manifestation of the morbid, unhealthy and disturbed thoughts you are allowing yourself to dwell on."

His mouth tightened but I went on, "You are either, I feel, using illness as a means of further dominating your wife or you are honestly making yourself ill by the negative thoughts you permit to fester in your consciousness."

No, love is not domination and occasionally I find myself explaining that fact in more outspoken language than I am accustomed to using.

On the other hand, love is not masochistic submission either. Love is bond, not bondage.

When I was a youngster there was a lady on our block, Mrs. Gerrity. She had a grown son who used to come home drunk regularly every Friday, pay night, and beat her up. It became a minor scandal in the neighborhood, of course, the more because Mrs. Gerrity had worked and brought up the son alone after his father died when the boy was still a child. People were always clucking and shaking their heads and saying, "It's a shame what he does to her, with her just worshipping the ground he walks on, the drunken bum. Some day he'll get his. Some day God will punish him for what he does to his mother."

They never said quite the same things to Mrs. Gerrity that they said among themselves because she wouldn't listen. Saturday mornings while "the drunken bum" slept off his hangover she'd sit outside on the front stoop, smiling bravely in spite of the black and blue marks on her face and body.

And when the women would stop by to talk she'd somehow manage to bring the conversation around to what a wonderful, wonderful son she had. How thoughtful he was. How he always took her to church on Sundays, never failed to remember Mother's Day and was forever bringing her home a pie or cake from the bakery where he worked.

And if anyone, someone who didn't know better, did dare to commiserate with her on those black and blue spots she would draw herself up and say proudly, "It's because he's had such a hard time of it, his father dying when he was no more than a poor baby. I'd never be one to blame him if he does get drunk now and again. I understand. And he's my son. I love him. More than my life."

To which the embarrassed commiserator could only say

with admiration something like, "You're a good, good woman, Mrs. Gerrity. You are a saint."

Did Mrs. Gerrity really love her son? Not many of us
would think of answering other than yes. Not many of us
would have the courage to answer other than yes, even if we
suspected that hers was a strange sort of love that permitted
such treatment. Once my answer too would have been an affirmative one but not since I began to realize that love, true love,
is based on mutual respect and mutual recognition of the
unique value of each part of the Whole. Yet love of any kind
often appears to be in such short supply in this world that
frequently we are only too ready, if not eager, to let all kinds
of other emotions hold themselves out in its guise.

The relationship between the Gerritys was not one of
love, on either side. Certainly it was an attachment and a very
strong one. And each was drawing from that attachment a
satisfaction that made it worthwhile. Son Gerrity was proving
himself to be what he believed himself to be—worthless—
and taking out on his mother his hate for the fate that had
made him fatherless, the next best thing to being able to punish fate itself. Mrs. Gerrity was quieting her irrational guilt
for her son's loss and at the same time gaining the praise-
worthy reputation throughout the neighborhood of being a
good, Christian woman, a martyr, a virtual saint.

Nor can it be called love when we attempt to hold onto
someone who no longer is or wants to be in our world. Painful as it may be on a human level we must accept the right of
another individual to cease to love us and to remove himself
or herself from our experience. To do otherwise, as a practical
matter, of course, can only continue the hurt and loss we feel
and will further act to shut us off from the possibility of a new
action of love in our life.

But, aside from the practical, if we insist on clinging to
a love that is dead we are selfishly insisting that we alone are
the one to be considered in a relationship that includes two,
that we alone are entitled to express our uniqueness as Love
in the way that we choose.

"Oh, you can talk!" I am often told tearfully when I try to get this point across in a counseling session. "I'll bet you've never had to go through anything like I'm going through. I'll bet you've never been rejected like I've been. I'll bet your wife (or husband or girl friend or boy friend) never left you for someone else."

And I have to assure the person that while it is true that I may not ever have gone through the same experience as he or she is presently going through—for example, I've never had a wife who's left me for someone else—but I've most certainly gone through a similar experience. I've been rejected. I've had to let people go that I didn't want to let go. I've known hurt and loss and pain.

"And I'm not telling you it's easy," I add. "No. I'm not telling you it's easy. It can be sheer hell. But there are ways to get through it. There are ways to make it easier."

Then I share with the rejected one some of the things that have helped get me through the rejections, the losses, the pains and hurts of relationships that have gone wrong.

Only yesterday a woman, Mrs. Keiller, came to see me at the urging of her children. She's in her late fifties and a year ago she'd married a man twenty years younger than she. Now he'd told her he was tired of her, wanted a divorce and had gone off with another woman, strangely no younger than she was.

I'd met the husband. He was a charmer but without much sense of responsibility.

"I won't let him go," she sobbed. "I love him and I won't let him go. I can't do without him. My children tell me that I was happy for nearly a year. That I had him for nearly a year and that it was fun and that now he's gone and I have to let him go. But I can't. I won't."

I watched her and my heart went out to her and it was very hard for me to say what I knew I had to say, "Your children are right, Mrs. Keiller. If he wants to go, you must let him go. It's wrong to try to hold on. Wrong and useless. Wrong, useless and far more painful than just letting him go."

"But why? He's my husband. We're married. Why should I let him go?"

"Well, I could say because you have no choice," I answered. "He's already gone. But I'm not talking about just letting him go in a physical sense. I'm talking about also letting him go in your mind. Setting him free emotionally. Setting yourself free emotionally. Setting him free to go to his new love emotionally as well as physically. Setting yourself free emotionally, to be open to a new love in your own life."

"But I don't want a new love." Her sobs increased.

"I know," I told her, "but he does. And if one person in a relationship no longer loves he or she should have the right to be free of it."

"Oh, I don't understand how you can say something like that. How about the other person? How about me?"

"I can say it not because the one rejected doesn't suffer. He or she does. Believe me, I know. I know what it's like. I've gone through it myself. More than once. But still I believe that each of us has the basic right to love and to have good relationships, your husband included. Each of us has the right to be fulfilled through love and good relationships, as we see love and good relationships."

"I just don't . . . ," she began.

"And to whatever extent we remain in a situation that no longer has them for us," I continued, "to that extent we rob ourselves of our basic right to them. And more, rob ourselves of the possibility of finding them with another. And that applies to you, Mrs. Keiller, as well as to your husband. Because if you try to hold him when he loves someone else, even if you do succeed—and you probably won't—he will not love you. He will not love you and you will not only be robbing yourself of your right to have love in that relationship but you will also be robbing yourself of the possibility—no, the certainty, if you want it—of finding a new love. Because you will not be open to the new, so long as you cling to the old."

For the first time she was no longer sobbing. Slowly she wiped her eyes and then sighed. "I've heard you say such things before," she finally said sorrowfully, "and I accepted them. I knew you were right. But then they didn't apply to me. Now they do. Yet, something inside me still knows you're right."

"Good," I said. "Now, shall I tell you some of the things that have helped me in a similar situation? Some of the things I've said to myself over and over again to help me get rid of hurt and loss?"

She nodded.

"Well, whenever a thought about the absent person comes to my mind, a mental picture or an incident in which he or she was involved, I stop anything I'm doing and I say—aloud and with great firmness if I'm alone; silently but with equal firmness if I'm not alone and someone else could hear— 'If you,'—meaning the absent one—'do not want to be in my physical world, you may not remain in my consciousness.'

"Now, of course, you know that what I'm doing is changing my own thought patterns, my own emotions about that person, don't you? I'm not really talking to the absent one, but to myself?"

Once more she nodded.

"Or I say to him or her—really, again, to myself—'You can no longer stay in my thoughts, taking up my time and energy. If you have removed yourself from my physical world, you may not take up my mental energy. I'll give my mental energy to the people who do want to be in my world.'

"And then I immediately say a treatment for myself. I treat myself for love. Love, love, love. Not love from a person at this point. Because usually that brings up the image of the absent one and a feeling of unrequited love. No, I just treat for love in general, love in the absolute. I say to myself, 'The Absolute Mind is Love. Where is the Absolute Mind? It is everywhere evenly present. And that means It is right where I am. Anywhere I move, I move into the action of love because love is to the right of me, to the left of me, before me, behind me, above me, beneath me, permeating me, radiating through me. I am one with the Infinite. The Infinite loves me because It created me and knows me to be one with Itself. I am one with the only One there is. I am one with First and Only Cause. There is no possibility of my being outside of Love because It is everywhere.'

"Again and again I repeat these or similar words to myself. Until I begin to feel my spirits lifting. Until I begin to feel and to believe that indeed I cannot be out of the action of love, that now when I seem to be is just a temporary condition, as all conditions are temporary, and that soon love in the form of another person will enter my life."

Some who are reading this book may think that the reason I advised Mrs. Keiller to let her husband go, the reason I believed he had the right to be free to go to his new love, was because I was taking into account the difference in their ages, that I thought the marriage between them unsuitable from the beginning and therefore that I saw no great grounds for keeping it intact.

But that fact had nothing to do with my reasoning. I am, I hope, not a moralist. I try not to judge or criticize or decide what types of people are suitable for each other in any kind of a relationship, be it an intimate one or simply one of friendship. Only the two people involved can make such a decision. But when I say the two people, I mean just that, the two people, not merely one of them.

Had the Keillers both been of exactly the same age my feelings would have been the same and my advice to Mrs. Keiller the same.

I remember a very young man who came to me a number of years ago. He was married and had two children but, he told me, he no longer loved his wife. He loved another girl and he wanted to divorce his wife and marry the other girl. His problem was that he was worried about what people would think, his and his wife's parents particularly, how the divorce might affect his job since his wife was a distant cousin of his boss, whether he would get to see his children often enough and other such matters.

I worked with him a number of weeks, trying to help him

straighten out his thinking so that he could see all the possible results of his contemplated action and decide intelligently whether he wanted and could handle those results.

After one session he turned to me as he was leaving and said, "I know you have an opinion about all this but you've never stated it and I'm grateful to you for that."

I looked at him, surprised. "But I don't have an opinion. Why should I? What makes you think I have?"

"Oh," he answered evasively, "you know. You're a counselor and all that. I'm sure you must hold the conventional, social view that no man should leave his wife and family."

"No," I said. "I don't hold any such view. Certainly I believe that any two people involved in a marriage—or any other relationship, even one of business, for that matter— should make every effort to work out their difficulties. But if they have honestly tried and one or both of them still feels there's no love—or compatibility in the case of the business partners—then I believe the relationship should be dissolved in order to leave each one free to find the love or compatibility which is his or her basic right."

"You believe in divorce?" he asked, astonished.

"I believe in divorce. Though, as I said, only after both parties have made a sincere effort to work out their relationship problems. I don't believe in divorce because one party likes a room hot and the other cold or because the two parties have had a tiff over the fact that one wanted to go to the movies and the other didn't. I believe in divorce when love is truly gone, on one side or both, and when one or both loves someone else and wants to be free to establish a new relationship of love and marriage.

"I believe, above all, in love itself, and that love holds together those who belong together and separates those who don't. I don't know your wife and I don't know the girl you want to marry. How then could I judge who belongs with whom? And even if I did know all three of you, I still wouldn't feel in a position to judge. Only those actually concerned in a relationship are in a position to make such a judgment."

"Thank you," he said. "You don't know how you've helped me. I don't feel so guilty any more."

We worked a number of weeks longer, he with increasing trust in me because I continued to keep my eyes firmly fixed on the goal of right relationships for all, regardless of the outcome.

And the interesting thing is that, in the end, his decision was to remain with his wife, though he'd not even considered such a possibility in the beginning.

But I'd made no attempt to influence him on any social grounds. He had come to see that, consistent with his own conscience, he could not be happy in another relationship if the second relationship required him to abandon his responsibilities to the woman he'd married and the children he'd fathered and she'd borne.

In his case, as in all others, the action of love, properly understood, held together those who belonged together and separated those who didn't; for the second girl soon would have become unhappy in a relationship where the man was unhappy.

I have another illustration, one that is slightly different from that of Mrs. Keiller, which shows the advisability of letting go of a relationship, both physically and mentally, when it is over.

A big, rugged man came to consult with me because he had suddenly found himself growing impotent with his wife. A disturbance in potency is difficult for one man to admit to another and Jim Sheldon stumbled embarrassedly through the facts of his case.

"It's my second wife," he told me. "We've only been married a couple of years and I love her very much. She's wonderful. Not like the first one. The first one turned out to be a nag and unfaithful in the bargain. I was glad to see her go. But this one — I don't want to lose this one and I'm going to if I can't make her happy.

"The thing is," he went on, "everything's okay when we begin to make love. I want to make love to her and everything seems okay and then she'll move in some way, do something, say something or look a certain way that for a moment reminds me of my first wife and all of a sudden I'm turned off. It's never the same thing and it's nothing she can help or does on purpose. Actually it's no one thing. Oh God, I wish it were. Then it would be something I could ask her to stop."

I could see the anguish on his face but I knew what he was doing so I remarked quietly that what he was telling me sounded a bit ridiculous. "After all," I said, "people are built much the same. Most of us have a head, a body, two arms and two legs, two eyes, a mouth, a nose, two ears and so on. It's irrational to expect that anyone can avoid occasionally moving or doing or saying or looking in a way that someone else has moved or looked or spoken. But if you realize that your second wife is not your first wife, that she is a unique expression of Infinite Intelligence, you should be able to stop the comparisons you're making, especially those to your first wife who is gone from your experience."

"I've tried. I really have," he answered. "Can't you help?"

"Well," I told him, "perhaps. If you'll consider engaging in a little experiment."

"Anything," he assured me. "Anything. Name it."

"I'd like you to phone your first wife, ask her to your home for next week-end and then I want the three of you, your first wife, your second wife and you, to spend the whole weekend together. And when I say together I really mean together. And that includes going to bed together."

I leaned back in my chair and waited for his reaction.

"Good Lord!" He let out his breath as if he'd taken a blow. "You can't be serious. I don't even know where my first wife is."

I continued to wait.

Finally he recovered enough to say, "I'm surprised that you'd suggest something like that to me. I mean, in your position. I'm surprised you'd suggest something so — so . . . . All I can think of is the word 'depraved'."

"But I must disagree with you," I said. "I didn't make the suggestion to you. At least I didn't make it first. You did. You long ago made the suggestion to yourself."

He frowned. "I don't know what you're talking about."

"Let me try to explain then. Don't you realize that your former wife might just as well be physically in your house, in your bedroom, in your bed, so long as you hold on to her in your thoughts as you do? In your mind, in your emotions she is in your bed. Unless you see what you're doing you'd be better off if she were actually physically in your house, in your bedroom and in your bed. You could then kick her out."

He sat there, staring at me. At last a light came into his eyes. "I see what you mean," he said, "and you're right. You're absolutely right. But what do I do now? How do I get her out of my thoughts, out of my emotions?"

"Where are thoughts?" I asked. "Where are emotions?"

"Where? I don't understand. In my mind?"

"Yes, of course, but that's not exactly what I mean. Thoughts and emotions are in the now. In the eternal now. Incidents, situations, conditions, people may be in the past but thoughts and emotions are always in the now. When we are thinking, when we are feeling, we are thinking and feeling in the now, not in the past. And when we know that, we also know that, whereas we cannot change the past so far as events, conditions, situations and people in it are concerned, we can definitely change the thinking and feeling we are doing about them right now. We can stop the way we are thinking and the way we are feeling by simply refusing to think and feel that way.

"Every time any thought of or any feeling about your former wife enters your mind, push it out. Think of something else. Immediately. Think of something you like about your present wife. Concentrate on how you feel about her, how much you love her. Be ruthless with yourself. Keep after yourself. Don't allow yourself the slightest deviation from this practice. Don't allow yourself even a momentary anger or hate, a momentary comparison. Never, never allow yourself to dwell on any memory of your former wife or on any emotion you have for her or may have once had for her."

"It doesn't sound so difficult when you talk about it," Jim said, "but I suspect it's going to be plenty difficult. Learning such absolute control over one's mind." And then he admitted, "I guess I do have a tendency not to want to let go of thoughts and feelings, especially when I'm upset or angry. All I can say is that I don't know if I can do it but I'm sure going to give it a hell of a try."

Did Jim Sheldon learn the control he set out to learn? Well, he's never discussed the matter again with me but the next time I saw him with his wife he gave me a big, boyish grin and a wink.

And Mrs. Sheldon was hanging onto his arm, looking very happy.

I am going to end this chapter with a meditation and a general treatment for love, a shortened version of one given at a noon meeting, again taped by a student. And, as before, when I arrive at the treatment part, I shall switch to the first person singular; so that, if you wish, you can use it for yourself:

Knowing that there's one Love, let's make ourselves acutely aware of this Love by imagining this entire room filled with It; by imagining that this Love is in every cell of our body and everyone else's body; that It is in every atom in the chairs, floor, ceiling, in every object and in the air surrounding us — which It is.

Knowing our bodies to be the action of Love and created by Love to house our consciousness on this earth plane, we love those bodies and we accept them as full of health and energy.

Knowing that our world of form and finance was created by Love to provide us with comfort, ease, pleasure and beauty, we love our homes, the food we eat, the clothing we wear, the transportation we take, the objects we use, the places where we work or visit in our leisure, and the resource called money, which, in our society, is used as a means of exchange for ideas, goods and services.

Knowing that our relationships with people are the cohesive action of Love that brings together all that belong together and separates all that do not belong together, we love the men, women, and children who belong to us by right of the consciousness within them and us and we wish well but let go of the men, women, and children who do not belong to us by right of the consciousness within us and them.

Knowing that the talents and abilities within us were given to us by Love for Its expression and for the expression of our individual self, we love them, accept them and share them with others with increasing joy and capability.

And in this total consciousness of Love let us think silently to ourselves:

"There is one Infinite Love and I am one with that Love. I am the manifestation of Love as, in and through me, right here and right now. Therefore I am one with every person, place and thing. I act only out of love. I project only love to every point in time and space. I attract only love. I am permeated by love. I am radiant with love.

"I release this treatment into the Law. The Law accepts it, acts on it and manifests it in my experience. And so it is."

CHAPTER XVII

Self-Expression — Using Talents
and Abilities to the Utmost

Essentially, we on this earth are constantly engaged in the process of dealing — or attempting to deal — with four basic human aspects of life: our physical, mental and emotional states (our body, mind and emotions), our world of form (objects, food, clothing, shelter, finances), our relationships with others (acquaintanceships, friendships, intimate associations), and our talents and abilities (those qualities inherent within each of us which the Infinite Intelligence gave us as a means of expressing our individuality—as a means of self-expression).

And in order to be happy, loved and loving, balanced, prosperous, healthy and creative, we must learn to deal successfully with all four of these aspects.

I doubt that many of us would consciously choose to be popular but the kind of person who can never get a job, has no money and is always sick.

And I doubt also that many of us would consciously choose to be healthy but poor, lonely and without creative ideas. In other words I doubt that many of us would consciously choose to be effective in any one or two, or even

194

three of the four aspects but deficient in the others or other.

Thus far I have discussed the first three aspects. Now I shall discuss the fourth, self-expression, the expression of our talents and abilities.

Many people who come to me for counseling come because they're dissatisfied in their work, can't find a job or can't get the job they want, need an interest or a hobby but aren't, they tell me, interested in anything particular or don't know what sport or what hobby they'd like to pursue. Or they're discontented with their appearance, the fashion in which they dress; their make-up and hair styling, if they're women. Or they're unhappy with the way they run their home, with their ability to create tasteful, efficient, comfortable and beautiful surroundings.

And when I tell them that what they're talking about is a failure to use their talents and abilities they look at me dejectedly and insist that they have no talents or abilities. Or if they do, they don't know what they are. Or they're not very great. Or anyhow, not great enough.

What they usually mean by such statements, though they're not aware of the fact, is that they're trying to meet the standards or expectations of some outside source, friends, parents, relatives, society, and neglecting to look within themselves for those gifts and attributes which are uniquely theirs and which, if used correctly, constantly nourished and improved, could bring them the joy, pleasure and sense of self-fulfillment they apparently lack.

Each of us has talents and abilities and these talents and abilities are no better, no worse, no greater and no smaller but merely different from the talents and abilities of everyone else. That is because the Infinite Intelligence which is the totality of all possibilities and which creates everything in order to express Itself never creates any two people or any two things exactly alike. Even so-called identical twins are never exactly alike, though they come from the same gene and it would seem impossible for them not to be exactly alike. No two snowflakes have ever been found that are exactly alike nor have any two fingerprints or voice prints.

Apparently the Absolute Mind does not duplicate and only produces that which It needs in order to express Itself fully. Therefore when you know that you are not and were not meant to be like anyone else and that you are a necessary part in the higher scheme of the Infinite Intelligence, you will lose your sense of competition and comparison.

You will know that your talents and abilities are yours alone, that they are needed, not only for your own self-expression but for the expression through you of the Cosmic Intelligence and that you cannot therefore be happy and fulfilled unless you know what your talents and abilities are, unless you are using them, unless you have found the place where they fit in and where you can contribute them and share them with others.

We can't all be bridge builders, millionaire executives, top-flight salesmen, best selling authors or the leading man or lady in the play of life. But it has been my experience that people are rarely critical or at odds with themselves if they are truly expressing their own individual talents and abilities.

Several years ago a young man came to see me and his first words, after telling me that his name was Glenn Levine, were, "I've been treating myself for a job. I've been out of work for a couple of months now and to tell the truth I know I'm resisting trying to find anything. I resent the fact that I have to work in order to survive."

He was dressed neatly, although not expensively. His hair was not extreme in cut and it was clean and combed. He looked neither lazy nor the kind of hippie who thinks the world owes him a living just because he happened to be born into it.

I suspected something lay behind his protest of which even he might not be aware so I said, "Nobody has to work to survive. Not these days. Not any more. Not in our society. You can always panhandle. You can get food somehow, if only by hanging around the automats like people did during the great depression and you can grab the remains of meals people leave on their trays. You can get your clothes from the Salvation Army and you can sleep under the eaves of Carnegie Hall in good weather and talk your way into some-one's crash pad in bad.

"If you want you can even fake insanity and the authorities will come and cart you off to Bellevue or Pilgrim State Hospital and if you don't mind losing your freedom and can keep the psychiatrists from finding out you're faking, you can stay in one place or the other until your days are ended. You can refuse to move and they'll carry you about. You can refuse to eat and they'll force feed you. You can refuse to bathe and they'll even bathe you. No, in this day and age and in this city, it's really not hard to survive without working."

"Well," he said, piqued, "I can't say that I appreciate your humor."

"Humor?" I answered. "I wasn't being humorous. You said you resent having to work to survive and I'm telling you that you don't have to work to survive."

"Yeah, I know. What you're really doing is passing judgment. Disapproving. Thinking I'm lazy and copping out. Well, maybe I am. But why should I work when I don't want to? I've only got one life. Why shouldn't I enjoy it? Why should I spend it doing something I don't want to do?"

"I'll buy that," I told him. "As far as it goes. Nobody should have to spend his life doing something he doesn't want to do. You don't want to work. Okay. What do you want to do?"

"Suppose I don't want to do anything? Suppose I just want to do nothing? Nothing at all?"

"Would doing nothing at all make you happy? Would you enjoy life doing nothing at all? Indefinitely?"

He stirred restlessly. "How do I know? I haven't done it long enough. Yes, I think so. At least I'm happier now than when I was working."

"You said you'd only been out of work a couple of months. What were you doing when you were working?"

"Selling insurance. Life insurance."

"And you didn't like it, I gather."

"No. I hated it."

"Did you ever stop to think that maybe it's not work in general you're resisting but that specific work — selling life insurance?"

"Sure. But I don't know what else I could do. I'm not trained for anything else. Oh, I know I've got to find a job eventually. In spite of your little speech I know I'm going to have to work to survive. I'm not the bum type. But that's the only reason. To survive."

"I still maintain, Mr. Levine, that you don't have to work to survive. You know what I think? I think what's really bugging you, what's really making you unhappy and restless is that something inside you that needs to be expressed isn't being expressed. And obviously also wasn't being expressed when you were selling life insurance either.

"You were born with certain talents and abilities, Mr. Levine. We all were; and you're not using yours. You're not expressing them and so you feel frustrated. You're not giving what you have to give so you're frustrating yourself and incidentally also depriving the rest of us of whatever it is you should be sharing and contributing."

"Oh, come off it," he answered. "I'm just an ordinary guy. I haven't got any particular talents and abilities. I mean, none that anybody needs or wants in any job I could get."

"I don't believe that's true."

"Okay, What are they? What are my talents and abilities?"

"I can't answer that. I don't know you well enough. But you can answer it. You can answer it, if you'll put some thought into finding out. Take a week or two. Apparently they don't lie in the direction of selling life insurance so you can rule that out.

"You see, it's really simpler than you think. People's

198

talents and abilities usually lie in the areas that interest them. The things they like to do and the things they do best and most easily — even if they don't realize it — they're enjoying and doing well and easily because when they're doing those things they're using and expressing their own individual talents and abilities. It sounds involved but I'm sure you understand what I mean."

"Yes, but . . . ."

"Let me finish before you 'but' me. A lot of people think that anything they can do easily can't be of much value. Or if they like to do something, have fun doing it, they feel guilty. They reason that if they're having fun it can't be work. And that's because we have come to think of work in terms of something we have to do; something that's boring or tiring or monotonous, a necessary evil if, as you put it, we want to survive.

"Think about what you really like to do. As I said, take a week or more, if necessary. If you find where your interests lie and can tie them in with some kind of job, I don't think you'll wince when you think of working. I love teaching, just as I once loved dancing and stage managing and producing. I wouldn't work at anything I didn't like. Not indefinitely. When I go to work, I go because I enjoy it, because it's fun."

"Oh, sure, but you do have talents and abilities. You don't have to try to figure out what they are. They're pretty obvious."

"Look, Mr. Levine, I've worked hard to be where I am. My talents and abilities may seem pretty obvious to you but they weren't so obvious from the beginning. I knew I liked teaching. I knew I liked seeing people learn and grow. But I had to find something I wanted to teach and I had to study and learn and practice and grow myself. So I'm not saying that when you do discover what you like to do and also do well that you're going to be able to get a job doing it right away. You too may have to study and learn and grow and practice. But because you'll be doing all these things in a field you like and for which you have inherent talent you'll enjoy them so much you'll forget they're really work."

Today Glenn Levine is building houses. He has his own company. It's small and he only builds one house at a time. But he always builds well, working along with the men he hires, using the best materials he can afford. Sometimes he sells his houses outright. Sometimes he only rents them. Last time I heard he was working seven days a week, but from choice and only because he loves what he's doing. I don't imagine he's getting rich fast but he's making out okay and he's happy.

After he left my office that first day he spent two weeks doing what I'd suggested, thinking about what he enjoyed doing. And all he could come up with, he told me the next time we met, was that he liked building things. He'd made all sorts of built-in drawers and cabinets and furniture for himself and his friends. In fact one of his proudest achievements was the bed-sitting room he'd designed and built for himself over the family garage when he was eight years old. He and his parents and his two sisters had just moved into a new house and the only space he could find just for himself was that space over the garage. And in order to get to it he'd even had to knock down part of the wall between the space and an upstairs bedroom and construct a doorway. Then he'd had to insulate the walls and put up wallboard. When all that was finished, he'd made himself a bunk bed and a built-in desk and chest of drawers.

Did Glenn Levine discover his talent for building and then go right out and start building houses? Hardly. He first had to go to trade school, then take on small jobs building rooms and additions and establish a credit rating so that he could get financing for projects of his own. The first house he built he lived in while he was building the second. Living in it, he discovered what he'd done right and where he'd made mistakes. When he built a third he moved into the second, selling the first, still learning by living in what he'd built.

Recently he built himself a combination home and office which I understand is quite a showplace and where, he tells me, he intends to stay put.

Working? He's not working he'll tell anyone. He's an eight year old kid having fun, having the time of his life.

We are always expressing ourselves whether we're doing it in business, at school, in the arts or crafts or in the home. And doubting one's talents and abilities isn't confined to people in or looking for a job. Only last week a woman, Diane Knolls, came to see me who described herself as "just a housewife."

I told her, smiling, that she sounded as though being a housewife were way down on the ladder of occupations.

"Well, most people think it is," she answered.

"I don't think it's important what most people think," I said. "What do you think?"

"I suppose I agree with them. I've been brainwashed too. Although actually I like it. I like being a housewife. Or I would if I were any good at it."

She paused, flushing. "I know you're going to think my problem is silly, Mr. Pace."

"Try me," I said. "I rarely think another person's problem is silly. Especially when I know it isn't silly to the other person."

"Well, you know, you're always talking about self-expression and how we're supposed to use our talents and abilities if we want to be happy and fulfilled but I don't seem to have any. We — my husband and I — we've been married three years and we've been living in a furnished apartment but now we've just bought a house. And the thing is I'm supposed to go out and buy some furniture and things to furnish it. Decorate it, I mean. Or whatever it's called. Anyhow, I don't know where to begin. I don't know what to buy. I get in an absolute panic trying to decide on what colors to have in the living room, what style furniture goes with what, what matches or blends with what and whether, if I buy this thing, it's going to clash with something else I've bought."

Again she paused. "I told you it's a silly problem."

"Let's stop characterizing it," I answered. "We're not going to get rid of it by characterizing it. In fact, characterizing it makes it seem to take on form when it's really just an idea. A mistaken idea. People's surroundings, people's homes, Mrs. Knolls, generally express themselves. Why don't you select what you like, what appeals to you, what expresses you? If you're having so much trouble making choices you must be trying to express someone else's likes and dislikes. You must be trying to meet someone else's standards and values. Whose? Your husband's? Why not get him to help you then?"

"Oh, no. It's not him. He doesn't care. I mean, if I ask him he'll give an opinion but he mostly leaves it up to me. It's just that — well, of course, I want it to look nice. The house. I want other people to think it's nice."

"What other people, if not your husband? What you choose some people are going to like and others aren't. No matter how you try. Now, I'm not saying that you shouldn't consult anyone. Or books and magazines about decorating. They'll give you ideas and help you to clarify what colors you do like, what styles do appeal to you, what things you do think go together. But ultimately, even if you were to hire a decorator, the choice is going to have to be yours. Yours and your husband's."

"But I don't have any faith in myself. I don't even know where to begin."

"Why don't you begin by going around to the various stores? Look at the model rooms. Try to decide what you like about them or don't like and why. Go to some second-hand book and magazine stores. Buy up a bunch of recent books and magazines on decorating the home. Study them. Mentally select what you like and try visualizing how what you select would look in your new home. Then when you've done all that you can and have time for, make your actual decisions. Trust your own instincts. Your own likes and dislikes. Your own talents and abilities. Whatever you finally choose will be right for you.

"Meanwhile, if you're not already doing so, begin immediately to give yourself treatments. Deny that you're frozen and can't make decisions. Affirm that you are full of confidence. That you do have talent and ability, that they are uniquely yours, given to you by the Absolute Mind in order for It to express through you. Affirm that you trust your talent and ability and know that they are equal to the task of surrounding yourself with the things that make for a home that is comfortable, efficient and beautiful.

"And as you go through the stores, looking at displays, or as you read the books and magazines for ideas on decorating, keep thinking about how much you enjoy being unique. How much you enjoy the opportunity to express your own individual talents and abilities. And once in awhile stop everything, close your eyes to shut out the world and say to yourself, 'It's great to be me. It's great to have my talent and my ability. It's great to be using them and sharing them. It's great to be expressing what I am. It's great to have a home and to be able to study and learn and improve the expression of me in it, the me that the Infinite Intelligence created me to be.'

"Will everything fall into place perfectly and will you make no mistakes? Perhaps. But more than likely you will find yourself regretting something you've bought, dissatisfied with how something looks, feeling you've made the wrong choice of something. But that's the way we learn and improve. And, as you know, no form is permanent. If you can't make an exchange, maybe you can eliminate or rearrange or dye or refinish or modify."

"You almost give me courage," Mrs. Knolls answered, drawing in her breath. "You almost make me believe I can do it."

"Of course you can. If you'll remember that it's your home. Yours and your husband's. You don't have to furnish it to suit anyone but the two of you. Suppose your parents don't like it? Or his parents? Or your friends? Or his boss? Or his boss's wife? It's not their home and who says any of them necessarily have better taste than you do? The horrors and discards of yesterday are the treasures and antiques of today. Be yourself. Trust your instincts and keep studying and learning."

She smiled. For the first time. "Does that apply to cooking too? I'm not a very good cook either."

"It applies to just about everything. Cooking can be as creative and self-expressive as building a skyscraper or inventing a new and better mousetrap. Pick up some cookbooks. Start experimenting. Fire up your enthusiasm by trying a new dish every day. Improve. Improvise. Throw out the failures and forget about them. Share the successes and get other people to share their successes with you. And remember, don't compare your cooking with anybody's. Not your mother's or your husband's mother's or the French chef's in the French restaurant where you once ate. You're you. And if you don't like the you that you are—well, that's what you're studying and learning for. To change you into a you that you will like. But meanwhile remember that your mother and his mother and the French chef didn't start out at the level they are now. And anyhow maybe you don't really like their cooking all that much. Maybe if you're yourself, you'll find you prefer your own cooking to theirs or anyone else's."

Before she left I gave her a treatment. It was weeks before I saw her again and then she told me that she was following my advice in detail. She was treating every day and she was waist-high in cookbooks and decorating books and magazines and she was studying and learning and practicing. Moreover she was loving every minute of it.

Diane Knolls is a good illustration of one thing I've learned about people who have trouble believing in their talents and abilities. If you can get them on the right track, get them interested and get them moving, they often end up succeeding in doing all sorts of things they never could have previously conceived of themselves as doing.

Now, when I tell you that self-fulfillment and contentment lie in using and developing your talents and abilities to their utmost, am I saying that if you don't like your job and feel it isn't using your particular talents and abilities you you should up and quit? Certainly not. You may need that job because you have responsibilities or because jobs of any kind at the moment may be hard to get or you may have neither the time nor the money to start all over, learning, studying and training in an entirely different field. You may have to stay where you are, for the present at least, and find an outlet for your talents and abilities in a hobby or avocation.

Or, if you're determined eventually to change your work, in spite of difficulties, you may have to study, learn and train for your new career in your spare time, while still holding down the job you're in. It's not always feasible or convenient to do what we want when we want to.

So, if for certain practical reasons of the moment you do decide you ought to stay in a job you don't like and where you feel your talents and abilities are being wasted, see if you can't dissipate some of your frustration by doing what you like to do, on the side.

I once knew a man who wanted to be a painter but he knew he couldn't earn a living for himself and his family by selling his paintings. People just weren't buying them. But he loved painting and couldn't give it up so he got a job as a night watchman.

He was a painter by day and a watchman by night. Eventually a few people did begin to buy his paintings but he could never sell enough to give up his watchman job. Still he was a happy man. He was meeting his responsibilities and doing so very well, after he began selling. He was also expressing the talents and abilities he had to the greatest degree possible.

Another thing to consider—if you're established in a job and feel you ought to stay there—is whether the talents and abilities you believe you have in another direction couldn't be adapted and used in some way right where you are. Many a person has discovered that when he (or she) looked at his work, not as something that had to be done for money (which

Don't Just Sit There—LIVE

is not to disparage money) but as a challenge, as an opportunity to see how much more productive, how much more interesting, how much more creative he could make that work, the work itself took on new meaning, gave greater satisfaction, even became so enjoyable it no longer seemed the same work. And, indeed, by that time it probably wasn't.

A friend of mine is head of a large concern and he frequently gives lectures on enjoying one's job and getting ahead in it. He says that one of the most important things is to watch with whom you pal around in the office, watch with whom you go to lunch. Are you palling and lunching with the gripers, the malcontents, the people who are forever criticizing management, the boss, their fellow employees?

If you are, he says, even if you liked your job to begin with, you're going to become dissatisfied with it soon. Even if you once enjoyed it, you're going to begin finding fault with it. Even if you do have talent and ability for what you're doing, you're going to begin to stop using that talent and ability, stop trying to improve, to learn, to grow.

And he urges the people in his audience to drop the faultfinders and complainers and to search out the employees who are enthusiastic, who like their work, who like the company, its officers and the others they work with. Or, he says, if you can't find anyone who's the company's booster, become that person yourself. You're not only likely to attract a following and thereby make the place a better one to work in, you're also likely to find increasing pleasure in what you're doing and get ahead rapidly.

One last thing I'd like to go into before I close this chapter and that is the problem of retirement.

Frequently, at a noon meeting, someone will send up a question about retirement. I remember one I received a week or two ago. It started out with the pathetic sentence: "I'm retired and I can tell you that retirement is hell!"

My answer to such a remark is, Yes, retirement can be hell because hell, to me, is a state of mind in which nothing creative is happening. So if you believe that when you have to retire at a certain age—and unfortunately in our culture many of us are forced when we reach the chronological age of 65 to retire from a job we may have held for years—that you also have to stop being productive, have to, in effect, retire from living as well, you are going to spend the rest of your life in that hell the person spoke about in the note.

But if you think of retirement as merely leaving something behind you no longer have to do, merely leaving something behind you're finished with as once you were finished with the first grade, grammar school, junior high and so on, then you'll realize that just because you've had to retire from a job, your talents and abilities aren't suddenly gone, haven't suddenly disappeared.

You can still produce something. It may be a product. It may be a service. It may be on a voluntary basis. I know people who have had to retire from one job and at that point found the courage to do something else they'd always wanted to do and not long after were just as busy in another job or business altogether and as happy as ever.

Here is a treatment you may find useful for improving your ability to express yourself:

There is one Infinite Intelligence, one Universal Mind and that Intelligence, that Mind is in, through and as all. Therefore It is in, through and as me. Its good is everywhere and I accept my good at the point where I am, right here and right now.

The Infinite Intelligence is never frustrated; therefore I am never frustrated. The Infinite Intelligence is always in right action; therefore I am always in right action. The Infinite Intelligence is always fully expressed; therefore, I am always fully expressed, in my home, in my work, in my hobbies and in my recreation.

I release this treatment to the law of cause and effect and it is demonstrated in my experience.

And so it is.

CHAPTER XVIII

The Ultimate Goal:

A Free Consciousness Living Creatively

Science of Mind makes no claim that if you study and understand and apply its teaching you will never again have another problem, another dilemma, another obstacle or another sorrow. What it does claim is that, through understanding its principles and applying the technique of treatment,
you will have fewer and fewer problems, dilemmas, obstacles
and sorrows as time goes on. And those you do have, you will
be able to deal with more effectively as you learn to control
your reactions to them. You will never again be overwhelmed
by anything because you know that all conditions are subject
to change through a change of consciousness and because
you also know that, in changing your consciousness and
thereby changing the conditions of your experience, you do
not have to depend only on the power of your own human
mind since you are one with the one great Power of the
universe.

And that is the concept on which Science of Mind is
based, the concept that you and I, that all people and all
things, are one with the great I AM, called Absolute Mind
in philosophy, God in religion and Order in science.

The Ultimate Goal: A Free Consciousness

Science of Mind is not a study of the human mind. That subject is in the field of psychology. Science of Mind is a study of the relationship between the human mind and the Universal Mind. And the relationship is one of unity, the human mind being part of the Universal Mind and producing or creating on the level of the finite as the Universal Mind produces or creates on the level of the infinite, both minds producing or creating in the same way — by thought.

The Universal Mind creates by thinking in and about and upon Itself, there being no other self, nothing else, for It to think in, about and upon since It is all. And when It thinks It conceives ideas of Itself, which through the Law of Itself — the law of cause and effect — creates form. And if our human mind is thinking correctly it too is thinking in and about and upon itself and conceiving ideas of itself which through the law of cause and effect become form.

And I say 'correctly' because most of us in Western culture are willing to do anything except go within ourselves and think within our own consciousness. Most of us spend our time thinking about what someone else thinks or wants or is doing. Therefore the ideas we conceive are someone else's ideas of us. Which means that we have lost sight of our uniqueness and of our responsibility to choose that which is right for us, that which is conducive to our peace, happiness, health, success, good relationships, self-expression and self-fulfillment.

The world of form is always effect, never cause. Experiences, conditions, relationships, situations, are all forms and therefore effects, not causes, or rather, not first causes, although you can make them secondary causes for future effects by constantly thinking about them.

All that materializes is form. So when you want to solve a problem what is the first thing you must realize? You must realize that all problems are effects, forms. And for every effect there was first a cause and the cause is usually some pattern of thought in your consciousness. When you realize that, then you have no choice but to discover the cause, the pattern of thought — if possible — and change it. And if you cannot discover the cause, then you must tell yourself and convince yourself that you negate the cause, whatever it is. That done, you immediately affirm the opposite — or whatever appears to you to be the opposite — state, effect, condition, to your problem.

Now this isn't, as I've said before, as difficult as it may sound. If you're sick and can't find the cause in some negative thought pattern in your mind, then simply deny that you have any thought patterns to create illness. Then affirm that you have only such patterns of thought as create health.

And keep on affirming, steadfastly and with conviction, in spite of any outward appearance to the contrary, that you have only such patterns of thought as create health until health does indeed materialize in your experience. Keep on affirming the cause you think is necessary to produce the effect you want in your experience.

And remember that in thought you are completely free. In thought there is no limitation, except the limitation you yourself place there. In thought there is no time and no space. Nothing and no one, except you, can stop you from thinking what you want to think. You can think of the past. You can think of the present. You can think of the future. You can think of a place called China or a place called California or a place called home and never move from your office chair. Your mother can't stop you from thinking what you choose, nor can your father, your wife, your husband, your background, your education or your lack of education.

So, however unpleasant your present circumstances, however unpleasant the effects that are the results of past causes, you are free, absolutely free in your consciousness, to change your patterns of thinking, to reconceive the ideas you hold of yourself, the people in your world and your experiences and then to impress the new conceptions on your consciousness until they are accepted and replace the old conceptions.

And when the old conceptions are replaced by the new,

the old, unpleasant circumstances will, indeed must, give way to new, pleasant ones.

In Science of Mind changing the consciousness is done, as you know, through the use of a technique we call treatment. For anyone who is not quite clear on what the technique is all about I am going to review the six steps by which I teach it. (Chapters V and VI present them more fully). Because it is through knowing the technique and how·it works that you realize that you don't have to will the new circumstances into being. You don't have to force the changes to come about. All you have to do is change your thinking, keep it changed, and the new circumstances will appear through the creative law of cause and effect.

The first step in treatment is to define the one great Power in the universe and you define that Power in whatever way has meaning for you — Infinite Intelligence, Cosmic Mind, First Cause, Life, Love, God. You define this Power in a statement that reminds you of what It is to you and of the fact that It is all. I usually think of It as Infinite Intelligence so I frequently begin a treatment by saying, "There is one Infinite Intelligence, in all, through all and as all."

When I was a beginner, back in my theatre days, in order to impress on my consciousness that the Infinite Intelligence was everywhere, equally present in its totality, I used to go around thinking to myself, "Infinite Intelligence is in the tree, in the swan on the lake, in the lake, in the coca cola bottle on the picnic table, in the picnic table, in the theatre, in the actors, in the script in my hand, in my hand." It helped me to see that whatever this great Power is, It is in, through and as all, not as an abstraction but as an ever present reality.

In step two of treatment you define yourself as this one great Power individualized or as the action of It. You are thus identifying yourself as part of It, as one with It. That does not mean that you are It in totality but that you are It at the point where you are. You have Its potential in human terms. I'd probably say, "And I am that Infinite Intelligence at the point where I am."

In step three you realize and declare to yourself that your good is available here and now. Many people have difficulty understanding this step because they forget that when they are giving themselves a treatment they are working in consciousness, not in the world of form. You must forget the world of form or conditions when you treat because continued awareness of the undesirable form or conditions you want to be rid of only serves to hinder you in achieving the complete change of consciousness, the complete change of cause, that can bring about a complete change in effect or result.

For this step I might say something like, "My good is available right here and now and I accept it."

In step four you deny any limiting form, any limiting condition, that remains in your consciousness, in spite of your effort to ignore it. If none remains then you can, of course, omit this step. In any case your denial should be brief. Don't dwell on the negative, even in denying it. For this step let's assume that I'm giving myself a treatment against a gall bladder attack and I have been unable to put its very present symptoms out of my mind. Knowing that Science of Mind and psychosomatic medicine agree that a gall bladder attack often results from extreme bitterness and deep depression, I'd probably say to myself something like, "I deny that I have any thought patterns of bitterness or depression in my consciousness."

In step five you affirm the thing you want. Sometimes I find myself thinking that this is the most important step of treatment and then I check myself, knowing that each step is equally important, although eventually some of them may become so much a part of your thinking that you may not have to state them in words. You may in time, for example, become so convinced that there is one Infinite Intelligence and that you are It individualized that you combine the two steps in one, as I often do.

Now, I want to remind you that in this fifth step of treatment, when you are affirming what you want, you are not just making positive statements. You are not just endeavoring to think positively. In Science of Mind treatment you are working in your consciousness to make total, permanent changes in the thought patterns which have been creating the undesirable or unpleasant effects in your experience.

So, if I were treating against a gall bladder attack, my affirmations might take this form: "I affirm that only patterns of happiness, joy and delight (opposites of depression), affection and love (opposites of bitterness) exist in my consciousness. And I affirm that I have a body that is always functioning perfectly in all respects and that I am therefore in a permanent state of perfect health."

In the sixth and final step you release your treatment to the creative law of cause and effect. You do this in order to keep clear in your mind that you do not have to make the demonstration or the result of your treatment happen. You do not have to force the effect you want. Effect will automatically come about from cause because that is the way the Law of Mind works.

Now, when I say you do not have to make the demonstration or result happen, I don't mean to give the impression that when a course of action is presented for you to take as a result of the treatment you can just sit there and not take it. Again I repeat, the Infinite Intelligence can only do for you what It does through you since It has given you the right of free will or choice.

At this point you may ask, as students of mine often do, how do I know when an action comes up that it's the one presented to me as a result of my treatment? How do I know that it's the right action? How do I know it's the one I'm supposed to take? How do I know, for example, that if I'm treating for the right job and a job is offered to me that it's the right job? And suppose I'm offered two jobs, how do I know which one to choose, which is the right one?

My answer to these questions is that usually your intuition will tell you. Usually you will sense what is right for you. But if you don't and can't, then make the choice that you believe is right and if it turns out not to be, then simply make another choice. Man is a choice-making animal. Exercise that gift. And don't be fearful. Be glad you have it. Because it is the means by which you can control rather than be controlled by events.

For step six I might say, "I release this treatment into the Law, knowing that the Law accepts it, acts on it and demonstrates it in my experience."

After you have released your treatment to the Law, it is good to add a final phrase such as "And so it is" because this further convinces you that your treatment is done and that your demonstration will therefore follow.

Having now reviewed the steps of treatment, at this point I'd like to review some of the Dos and Don'ts of treatment.

1. When working to improve yourself, try to find the causes — mental equivalents — of your troubles.
2. One treatment can make the change you seek, and immediately, but sometimes the time it takes for us to accept a new idea results in delay between treatment and manifestation. Therefore, repeat a treatment as many times as it takes until the trouble or problem disappears or is solved. A treatment is successful only when one has achieved the results he or she wants.
3. Don't let treatments become ritualistic. Vary them. Try to put progressively intensive emotion into them.
4. Treat away any doubts or fears that crop up by giving yourself a treatment for doubts and fears.
5. If doubts and fears persist, shift your attention to something else.
6. Don't wait for a 'quiet time' or a specific time; treat problems the moment they appear.
7. Use treatment as a way of life to improve constantly the quality of your lifestyle.
8. The Law of Creativity (cause and effect) is a natural law like the Law of Gravitation. Regard it as such.

9. The principle of attraction recognizes that each of us is surrounded by an atmosphere created by our predominant thoughts and feelings. That atmosphere attracts what our mind projects. Project, therefore, only what you want to attract.

If you've been giving yourself treatments for something for some time and the solution to your problem hasn't yet appeared, these considerations may be of help. The Law works for all alike. If your good doesn't manifest, try to discover what you're doing or failing to do that could be responsible for your seeming lack of results.

1. Are you nullifying your treatments by indulging, immediately after giving one, in an opposite thought or emotion?
2. Are you letting worry negate your affirmations?
3. Are you keeping your mind on the affirmative idea?
4. Are you confusing your consciousness by constantly changing your goals?
5. Are you glibly treating for something you only half want?
6. Are you unwilling to give up the attitude or condition that's holding back the demonstration?
7. Are you thinking of the Power in human terms?
8. Are you seeing yourself and your potentiality in relative rather than absolute terms?
9. Are you remembering that it's on the absolute plane, usually not the relative, that all good is available immediately?
10. Are you lingering so long on the denial that you are giving power to the negative?
11. Are you so intent on the literary style of your treatments that you lose sight of their meaning?
12. Are you outlining the solution of your problem, masterminding the cosmos, rather than relaxing and letting it happen?

13. Are you worrying about your treatments rather than releasing them to the Law with confident expectation?

14. Are you forgetting that nothing can happen to you that doesn't happen through you and are you failing to take the action that is presented to you as a result of your treatments?

Many people see in Science of Mind merely a day to day problem-solving discipline and a method for acquiring health, success, good relationships and money. And that's all right, as far as it goes. No one wants to have problems and I have no fault to find with anyone's wanting to obtain the material things of this earth for they too are manifestations of the Infinite Intelligence.

But when these same people fail to realize that in Science of Mind and the technique of treatment, they also have the means whereby they can achieve an inner consciousness that, in its peace, order, harmony, love and creativity, is akin to the Cosmic Consciousness, then they are missing the very essence of the teaching.

But to achieve such a consciousness we must be free not only of the negative thought patterns and emotions that are currently bothering us, we must also be free of all the human-race mind misconceptions we may have been taught about race, color, religion, age, sex and nationality, as well as the personal insecurities, hates, angers, envies, bitternesses and jealousies of the past. Because while they may not be troubling us at the moment, they are always potential trouble-makers and keep us from attaining the best of which we are capable. And finally we must never forget to introduce into our consciousness new, positive, creative thought patterns and emotions in place of the old, negative, stultifying ones we are eradicating.

I have a long combination meditation-treatment, some version of which I use at least twice a year — much as I might give my apartment a thorough housecleaning — for clearing my consciousness of any vestiges of past misconceptions and negative thoughts and emotions and of any new ones I may have unconsciously acquired in the interim between the two treatments. It has been of value to me and I know that it has also been of much value to many of my students so I am going to end the book with it:

Whatever Life is, It is everywhere and It is timeless. And my life and your life are some part of the Life that animates the universe. And so you and I cannot be hindered, handicapped or limited in our expression because through us Infinite Intelligence lives and expresses and creates. Its work is complete and perfect and since my life and your life are part of Its life, they too are complete and perfect.

And so we're going to go through our lives, period by period, from time immemorial up to right now and let go of anything that is in any way deterring or hindering or delaying our good from demonstrating where we are.

We can't prove or disprove that you and I lived somewhere before, that we had previous lives as some people believe. But maybe we did exist as an idea. I don't know. But anyway let's for a moment imagine that we were somewhere before we existed on this plane of action. And let's now free ourselves of any guilt, any hurt, any resentment, any negative thought or feeling of any kind we might have had then. Let's forgive ourselves for them. And let's also forgive any person, place or thing that might have caused or helped cause them.

So whatever existed, if anything did, to trouble us before we came to this plane of action, we are now absolutely free of and liberated from it. It is eradicated from our consciousness.

And let's think now of the physical preparation to come into our world, of the moment of conception, through the entire gestation period of about nine months, to the moment of delivery. If during this period you and I picked up any negative, we now let it go. And if we think that any person hurt us or caused a problem for us during this period, we now forgive him or her and expunge the matter or matters from our consciousness, whether or not we have ever had any memory of them. And if through our preparation to come into our world, we created a problem or a negative of any kind for any other person — fear, insecurity, resentment — we forgive ourselves and expunge these too from our consciousness.

So from time immemorial to the moment when we were born, we are absolutely free and there is nothing but love in our experience. In us, for all of this period, there is a sense of love for every person, place and thing, including ourselves, a deep sense of love for the thing we are and for the thing they are.

And now let's think about the time from the moment we were born until we were about two years old, the baby, the infant, the toddler. And again, if during this period we created any negative in any person's mind, we set that person free of it and we forgive ourselves. And if during this period any person created in our mind a negative, perhaps rejecting us, causing us fear, comparing us unfavorably to someone else, we forgive that person and we efface the negative or negatives from our consciousness.

And so from time immemorial until we were two years old, we are absolutely free of all negatives. We feel only love, freedom and a great sense of creativity.

Now let's move in our minds from the period when we were two until we were just about to go to school, around six in this country, the period in which we were beginning to learn more about the social environment in which we lived and therefore a period in which we could have picked up many misconceptions. And if we did, we now let them go and we place no blame against any person, place or situation that may have taught them to us. We realize that no one ever harmed us permanently. Infinite Intelligence never permits any part of Its creation to be harmed permanently. Even if we believe that someone treated us meanly, spitefully or viciously, we forgive him or her. We give up judging. We set him or her free. And if during this period, we ourselves harmed anyone or created a problem for anyone, we forgive ourselves and set ourselves free.

So from time immemorial until we were six years old, we are absolutely free, absolutely happy and full of love.

Now let's move to the time when we were in grade school, from about six until about thirteen, a period of awakening, of learning, of growing up, and hence a period when perhaps we picked up resentments or angers or beliefs that we were inferior or superior to others. If so, we neutralize these emotions in our consciousness and we forgive anyone who might have contributed to our acquiring them. We give up judging. We give up condemning. And if we injured anyone, caused anyone hurt or pain, we forgive ourselves. We do not condemn ourselves either.

So from time immemorial until we were thirteen, we are free of resentments, hates, fears, angers, comparisons and guilt, free of all negative thoughts and emotions. For these years we have only a consciousness of contentment, of inner security and of harmony.

And now we move from the age of thirteen to the age of twenty-five, a period when many of us begin forming close relationships with the opposite sex and thus a period when we might have encountered slights, rejections, emotional wounds. If we did, we forgive all who contributed to these pain situations and we forgive ourselves if we slighted, rejected or emotionally wounded another or others. Whether or not we remember all or none of these incidents, we erase them totally from our consciousness, ending the possibility of their ever again affecting us.

So from time immemorial until we were twenty-five, we are absolutely free. In our consciousness for this interval, we have only love, compassion and understanding.

And now let's move from the period of twenty-five to the present. And again, whether or not we can recall the circumstances, if during this time anyone caused us unhappiness or if we caused anyone unhappiness, we forgive him or her and we forgive ourselves. We are no longer emotionally attached to anything but happiness for these years.

So from time immemorial to the present, we are free of all negative patterns of causation, free of all misconceptions. Therefore we are secure, confident, loving, understanding and happy.

There is one Cosmic Mind, one Infinite Intelligence, one Life Force, one great Power and one Love, in, through and as all. Therefore I am that Mind, Intelligence, Life Force, Power and Love individualized at the point where I am, here and now.

From this moment I am free of all negatives, all human-race mind misconceptions, and I move forward in perfect health, perfect self-expression, perfect prosperity, perfect love, perfect creativity, perfect peace and perfect happiness.

I release this treatment into the Law. It is accepted and demonstrates in my life.

And so it is.

Betty Bailey

26081 Mocine Av

Hayward

886-5335

Home: 887 7120